I0528541

THE ETERNAL GODHEAD

EXPLORING THE TRINITY, CREATION, AND DIVINE WILL

PETER MARTYR VERMIGLI

MONERGISM BOOKS

CONTENTS

CHAPTER ONE

OF THE NAME OF JEHOVAH, AND OF SUNDRY ATTRIBUTES OF GOD

The nature of God is infinite, so as it cannot be comprehended under one title to know him by; wherefore his name is very large: yet nevertheless, by effects and works are gathered his singular properties, whereby we may understand all the divine nature and power, that seeing we cannot comprehend the whole, we may at the leastwise come unto the knowledge of him by parts. If there were any so rude and unskillful, as he knew not the value of a double sufferant, we would say that the same containeth in it, pence, grotes, testers, shillings, crowns, nobles, royals, and lastly, the sum of twenty shillings. By these parts and small portions, unless he were exceeding blockish, he might understand how much a double sufferant is worth. Even so men, after a sort, do perceive the nature and infinite substance of God by these parts and titles to know him by, not that there be any parts in God, but because that we only by such effects and parts may gather of his power and infinite greatness. Divers and manifold are the titles, whereby he is known: as when he is called Pitiful, Merciful, Constant, Just, Good, The God of Sabaoth, and such like.

2. And that this may be the better understood; he is called Jehovah of Haia, that is, To be: and that name agreeth properly unto God. For God is so an essence or being, as the same floweth from him unto all other things. Whatsoever things are, do depend of him, neither can they be without his power and help. Lastly, they have also promises of him, both to be, and to be performed. Wherefore that name of Jehovah is properly attributed unto God: of the similitude of which word, Jupiter being desirous to be reputed for a God, commanded himself to be called Jove. The Rabbins say, that those letters, whereof that word consisteth, are spiritual. And undoubtedly, God is a spirit; and a spirit first signifieth things that be without bodies, or that have light bodies, as vapors and exhalations, the which in show are light and thin, but yet they are of exceeding great strength. For by them, earthquakes are stirred up, the huge seas are troubled, the storms of wind are blown abroad. Wherefore that word began afterward to be applied to the soul of man, to angels, and to God himself: for these things, which otherwise seem but slender, do bring great things to pass. Others say, that those letters, whereof the word Jehovah is written, be resting letters: and that is very agreeable unto God. For seeing we do all seek for rest and felicity, there is no way to find the same, but in God only; thus much hitherto of the word. Jehovah signifieth the chief being; whereupon Plato had that his <H&G>, or essence. And that this may be the more manifest: some of the names

of God are derived from his substance, and other from some property. Substantial names be Jehovah and Ehi: that word signifieth, I will be. For there is no creature that may say; I will be. For if God draw back his power, all things do straightway perish. God doubtless may truly say so, because he cannot fail nor forsake himself.

Other names are referred to some property of God; as El unto might, Cadoseh unto holiness, Schaddai unto sufficiency: howbeit these things in God be no accidents, but only as we comprehend them in our cogitations. For whereas God is infinite, and we cannot wholly comprehend him; yet by certain tokens and effects we do in some part understand of him: thereof are those names, which signify some property of God. The Jews being led of a certain superstition, pronounce not that holy name Tetragrammaton, but in the place thereof they put Adonai, or Elohim; and so think that they worship the name of God more purely and reverently: but God requireth no such kind of worship. And hereby it cometh to pass, that in translating of the holy scriptures, the Grecians for Jehovah have made Lord: as, instead of Jehovah liveth, they have said; The Lord liveth. And whereas in the New Testament Christ is so oftentimes called Lord, his Godhead is nothing at all excluded by that word, as some impure men do babble, but is rather established. Undoubtedly Thomas joined both together; My Lord (saith he) and my God.

Finally, God, to the intent that the knowledge of him might not be forgotten, hath accustomed to put men in mind of those benefits, which he hath bestowed upon them; and would that those should be as certain words expressing unto us his nature and goodness. And he beginneth always the rehearsal at his latter benefits; and of them he claimeth to himself titles or names attributed unto him, under which he may both be called upon, and acknowledged. For even at the beginning, God was called upon, as he which had made heaven and earth; afterward, as he that was the God of Abraham, Isaac, and Jacob; after that, as the deliverer out of Egypt; then a deliverer out of the captivity of Babylon: but lastly, as the father of our Lord Jesus Christ.

Of the omnipotency of God, look Peter Martyr in his Treatise, Of both natures in Christ, set forth at Tygure.

3. The words which be in the second book of Samuel, the seventh chapter, verse the 23, namely, The gods came that he might redeem unto himself a people, are a sharp corsie unto the Hebrews, which will not acknowledge three persons in the divine nature. Some, because it is said, God's, refer it to the opinion of men. Such is that saying of Paul; There be many gods, and many lords. For neither can they admit or allow of a multitude of gods. But forsomuch as the entreating here is of a singular or particular fact, this place must in any wise be understood of the true God. Kimhi thinketh, that David said, God's, for honor sake; even as men also, to speak the more pleasingly and civilly, do oftentimes use the plural number, instead of the singular. But if it be so, what new religion entered straightway into David? Why did he straightway add; Thou Lord, in the singular number? For we must heap upon God all the honors that we can. Others had rather refer this saying unto Moses and Aaron, who were sent to deliver the people out of Egypt: but this cannot be; for in the book of Chronicles, all these things are spoken of God himself by name. For so David speaketh; Thou camest to redeem thy people. Wherefore we shall much more rightly and truly understand the three persons in one divine nature; namely, the Father, the Son, and the holy Ghost: which being three persons, yet are they shut up under one substance. This opinion is true, sound, and catholic, whether the Hebrews will or no.

But those words, which be added; And might do great things for you: some would by Apostrophe or conversion of speech, refer them to the Jews, which me think is not probable. For David talked not of these things with the people, but secretly with God. Wherefore I had rather thus to understand them of God himself, and to ascribe these marvelous things to one God in three persons. But God came to deliver his people, when he sent Moses and Aaron unto them: for when he appointed Moses to that message, he added withal; And I will be with thee. God doubtless is in every place at all times; but then he is said to come, when he doth some great or new thing. And so he was said to be among the Jews, when he smote the Egyptians and their first borne. Again, when Pharaoh followed the Jews going forth of Egypt, and that they began to murmur, thinking that they should even then have perished, Moses on this wise recomforted them; God shall fight for you, and ye shall be still: yea the Egyptians themselves also did perceive the same. For they said; Let us fly away, for God himself doth fight for them. Yea and afterward, when the people had worshipped the golden calf, and that God was angry, he would not go forth with them, yet Moses entreated him to go on with them. Wherefore to deliver the people, there came both the Father, and the Son, and the holy Ghost. And although those works were common unto the three persons, yet are they severally and particularly ascribed to the Son. And therefore Paul saith unto the Corinthians, that that rock, from whence the water did flow, was Christ; And let us not tempt Christ (saith he) as some tempted him in the desert. By which words of Paul, we manifestly gather; that the Jews murmured against Christ. Which being so, the Arians may be very well confuted by that place. For if it were Christ, as doubtless it was, (which came to redeem the people) how can David say; There is no other God as thou art, if the Son be either a creature, or inferior to the father? For although this argument bind not the Jews, who receive not Paul; yet doth it bind the Arians, which cannot refuse Paul.

4. But the testimonies, whereby we prove the divinity of Christ, are taken as well out of the old, as out of the New Testament. Matthew saith; that We must baptize in the name of the Father, of the Son, and of the holy Ghost: In which words he showeth, that there be three persons coequal one with another. And we read in John; This is life everlasting, to know thee, the only true God, and Jesus Christ whom thou hast sent. Neither might Christ be called the first and principal good, or else eternal life, unless he were God. When the high priest had demanded of Christ with admiration, whether he were the son of the living God? The Lord answered him; Thou hast said. The which he hearing, rent his garments, and understood that he affirmed himself to be God. Furthermore, very firm is that saying; And God was the word: especially seeing it is added a little after; And the word was made flesh. Where thou seest, that the subtle argument of the Arians taketh no place, whereby they affirm, that Christ no doubt was called God, but yet that he was not so indeed: whereas John saith most plainly; that The word was God, and was made flesh. Further we read in the same John; that No man hath seen God at any time, but the son which is in the bosom of the father, he hath declared him. In which place thou hearest, that the son of God is exempted from the common condition of men. It is said by the same John; All things are made by him. Upon which place Augustine doth very well infer, that the son of God was not made: for if he had been made, then all things that were made, had not been created by him; at the leastwise he had been created by another thing.

Thomas, when he had seen the gashes where the nails entered, and the open wound of Christ his side, he spake forth allowed; My Lord and my God. Also Christ prayed to his father saying; Glorify me, O Father, with the glory, which I had with thee, before the world was made: which saying might not stand, unless that Christ had the divine nature; for his human nature was not before the world was made. Also the Lord said; All things that my father hath, are mine: and that the father hath the divine nature, it is by none called in question; and so of necessity the son is not without the same. Besides, Christ testifieth and saith; All things that my father doth, I also do: but the action of them both, being all one, the natures of them must needs be one and the same. He said to the Jews; Before that Abraham was, I am: which cannot otherwise be referred but to his divine nature: and no less do these sayings prove; I am the resurrection and the life. Again; As the father hath life in himself, so he hath granted to the son to have life in himself. Hereby it is proved, that the son is equal to the father. And the same John wrote in his first epistle, the fifth chapter; And we are in him that is true: that is, in his son Christ, which is very God, and eternal life. Our savior said to Nicodemus; No man ascendeth into heaven, but he that came down from heaven, even the son of man, which is in heaven. And Christ was not in heaven, while he talked with the Jews, unless it were as touching his divine nature: neither did he descend out of heaven, but in respect that he was God. Of which coming down, he again testifieth, when he saith; I came down from heaven, not to do mine own will, but the will of him that sent me. Again, I came out from my father, and I go unto my father.

5. All these things must be referred unto the divine nature. In the Apocalypse also he testifieth, that he is alpha and omega, The first and the last. And in the same book, the 19th chapter, it is written of Christ, that there was written upon his thigh, and upon his garments, King of kings, and Lord of lords. And least thou shouldst imagine, that that little, was the Epitheton ascribed unto God, there is mention made in the seventeenth chapter of the lamb himself; that He had the victory,

because he was the King of kings, and Lord of lords. Which property, that it belongs only unto God, it is manifest by the first epistle of Paul unto Timothy, where, towards the end of the epistle, it is written; Until the appearing of our Lord Jesus, which he shall show in due time, that is blessed, and Prince only, the King of kings, and Lord of lords. To the Romans he saith; Of them came the fathers, of whom, as touching the flesh, Christ came, who is God over all, blessed forever. Besides, when it is commanded; Thou shalt worship the Lord thy God, and him only thou shalt serve. It is said by Paul unto the Philippians; In the name of Jesus, let every knee bow, both of things in heaven, of things in earth, and things under the earth. And to the Hebrews; When he bringeth his son into the world, he saith, Let all the angels of God worship him. And in the same place, out of the sentence of the psalm, the power of creating is attributed unto him; And thou Lord in the beginning, didst lay the foundation of the earth. There is also another psalm alleged; Therefore hath God, even thy God anointed thee with oil of gladness above thy fellows.

And there is a comparison of Christ with Melchizedek, namely, that they were both without father, without mother, and without genealogy; which thing accordeth not with Christ, but so far forth as he is God. Unto the Colossians we read; that In Christ dwelleth all the fullness of the godhead bodily. Again; All things are made by him, whether they be things visible or invisible, or thrones, or dominions. Unto Titus; We expecting the blessed hope, and coming of the glory of the great God. Here Christ is most plainly called The great God. And in the second to the Corinthians; When he was rich, he was made poor for all men. It cannot be meant that he was rich, but in respect of his divine nature. And in the first epistle to the Corinthians; If they had known him, they would never have crucified the Lord of glory. And in the eight chapter;

To us nevertheless there is one God, which is the father, of whom are all things, and we in him; and one Lord Jesus Christ, by whom are all things, and we by him. But if that all things are by him, verily there is no doubt, but that he is God. And unto the Galatians, as touching the time of infidelity, it is written; When as ye served those which in nature be no gods, &c. By which words, the contrary is gathered; that seeing they were converted unto Christ, and served him, they served him that in nature is God.

But to follow the sure and more undoubted testimonies of the Old Testament, out of David we have; The Lord said unto my Lord, Sit on my right hand, until I make thine enemies thy footstool. Isaiah calleth him Immanuel. And again he saith; His name shall be called Wonderful, a Counselor, God, &c. Jeremiah in the 21st chapter, saith, that he must be called God our righteousness, and he useth the name Tetragrammaton. The very which thing thou mayest see to be done by the same Prophet, in the 31st chapter, wherein, though he speak of the city, I mean of the people of God, or of the church; yet nevertheless, all that doth appertain unto Christ, which is the head of the same: yea rather by him is such a name attributed to the church and people of God. Also we read in Isaiah; Who shall be able to reckon his generation? And in the Prophet Micah; And thou Bethlehem of Jewry art not the least among the thousands of Judah: for out of thee shall come forth unto me, one that shall rule my people Israel, whose out-going hath been from the beginning, and from everlasting: by which words, both the natures of Christ are showed. Add again out of the Prophet Isaiah, that which is cited by Paul in the 15th chapter to the Romans; There shall be a root of Jesse, which shall arise to rule over the Gentiles, and in him shall the Gentiles trust. And certain it is, that he is to be accursed, which putteth any hope in a creature. Therefore, seeing we must put our trust in Christ, and that he is to be called upon, it plainly appeareth that he is God. There might be heaped up other testimonies of this matter, but these I think to be enough, and enough again, to confute the boldness of these men.

Whether the holy Ghost be God.

6. Now it shall not be from the purpose, to confirm by many reasons, that the holy Ghost is God. This word spirit, sometime signifieth a certain motion, or a nature moveable; sometimes it is taken for life, or mind, or the force of the mind, whereby we are moved to do anything; it is also transferred to the signifying of things, which be separate from matter, as be the angels, which the philosophers call Intelligences: yea, and it is so far drawn, as it representeth our souls. Which metaphor seemeth to have respect thereunto, because we sometimes signify by this name, the thin exhalations, which breath either from the earth, from the water, from the blood, or from the humors of living creatures: which exhalations, although they be not easily perceived by the sense, yet are they effectual, and of exceeding great force; as it appeareth by winds, earthquakes, and such like things. And so it cometh to pass hereby, that the name of these most subtle bodies, whose force is exceeding great, hath been translated to the expressing of substances without bodies. Wherefore it is taken for a word general, both unto God, unto angels, and unto our souls. And that it is attributed unto God, Christ showeth, when he saith; God is a spirit, and thereupon concludeth, that he must be worshipped in spirit and truth. When it is so taken, this name comprehendeth under it, the Father, the Son, and the holy Ghost. But sometime it is taken particularly; for the third person of the Trinity, which is distinct from the Father and the Son. And of this person we speak at this time, wherein two things must be showed: first, that he is a person distinct as well from the Father as the Son: secondly, we will show that the holy Ghost is by this mean described to be God.

7. As touching the first, the apostles are commanded in the Gospel, that they should baptize in the name of the Father, of the Son, and of the holy Ghost. Which place doth most plainly express the distinction of the three persons, and doth signify nothing else, but that we be delivered from our sins, by the name, power, and authority of the Father, of the Son, and of the holy Ghost. And in the baptism of Christ, as Luke rehearseth, the voice of the Father was heard, which said; This is my beloved son, &c. Further, the holy Ghost appeared under the form of a dove. Here, as thou seest, the Son is baptized, the Father speaketh, and the holy Ghost showeth himself in form of a dove. In John it is said; I will ask my Father, and he shall give you another Comforter. Here also the Son prayeth, the Father heareth, and the Comforter is sent. And again; He shall receive of mine: whereby is signified, that the holy Ghost doth so differ from the Father and the Son, as he is derived from both.

And least that any man should think, that when Christ promised that the holy Ghost should come upon the believers (as in the day of Pentecost it came to pass) only a divine inspiration and motion of the mind was signified, the words of Christ are against it, wherein he said; He shall teach you all things, and bring all things to your remembrance, which I have told you. But inspiration and motion of the mind, do not teach nor prompt anything; but are only instruments, whereby something is taught and prompted. And the action of teaching and prompting, cannot be attributed but unto one that is a person indeed. Which is proved by other words of Christ, when he said of the holy Ghost; He shall speak whatsoever he shall hear. And that this third person proceedeth from the Father and the Son, it is evident enough in the same Gospel of John, where it is written; When the Comforter shall come, whom I will send unto you: even the Spirit of truth, which proceedeth from the Father. Seeing the son saith, that he will send the Spirit, and (as we said before) affirmeth him to receive of his; no man doubteth, but that he proceedeth from the son. And he now expressly addeth; Who proceedeth from the Father.

8. Now have we first declared out of the holy scriptures, that the person of the holy Ghost is distinguished, as well from the Father as the Son; and that he proceedeth from them both. Now must we see, whether he be God. This doth Paul show two manner of ways: first, when it is said; There be diversity of gifts, but one Spirit; diversity of operations, but one and the same God. But to give gifts and spiritual faculties, is no whit less, than to distribute operations: wherefore, seeing the holy Ghost is said to distribute gifts, and God to impart actions unto men, it is manifest that the holy Ghost is God. If the spirit be the author of graces, and the Father of operations; it is meet that the holy Ghost should be equal to God the Father. Further it is added; that The same spirit doth work all these things, distributing to everyone even as he will. Seeing then the sovereign choice is in him, to impart heavenly gifts, he is God. And it is written; Ye are the temple of God, and the Spirit of God dwelleth in you: if any man do violate the temple of God, him shall God destroy. But it is not meet for any creature to have a temple, seeing the same is proper unto the divine nature. Wherefore, seeing we be called The temples of the holy Ghost, it is now manifest, that he is God.

And least we should think it lawful to build temples unto martyrs, let us hear Augustine, who denieth that we build temples unto martyrs; we build them (saith he) unto God, although they be called The memories of martyrs: and out of Augustine himself is this form of reasoning gathered. Neither did the apostle but only once say; that We are the temples of the holy Ghost, but he hath the very same thing in the sixth chapter of the same epistle, where it is written; And do ye not know that your bodies are the temples of the holy Ghost? Furthermore the power of creating, which is proper unto God, is ascribed unto the holy Ghost; seeing David hath written; By the word of the Lord were the heavens made, and all the powers of him by the spirit of his mouth. And again; Send forth thy spirit, and they shall be created, and thou shalt renew the face of the earth. And in Matthew it is said of the body of Christ, which should be brought forth in the virgins womb; That which is borne in her, is of the holy Ghost. Again; The holy Ghost shall come upon thee, and the power of the most high shall overshadow thee. Seeing then the holy Ghost hath the power of creating, (as it hath been declared) undoubtedly he is God.

In the same epistle to the Corinthians it is said, that he searcheth the bottom of God's secrets: and it seemeth that the apostle maketh this kind of argument; The things which be of man, no man knoweth, but the spirit of man which is in him: even so the things that be of God, none knoweth but the spirit of God. And so he will have it, that even as the spirit of man is unto man; so the spirit of God is towards God. And no man is ignorant, but that the spirit of man belongeth unto the nature of man; whereby it is certain, that the spirit of God is of his divine nature. Basil against Eunomius useth another reason, which cometh in a manner to the selfsame; he saith, that the holy Ghost is the spirit both of the father and of the son, and therefore of the very same nature that they be. For it is written in the epistle to the Romans; And if the spirit of him, which raised up Jesus from death, do abide in you, he that raised up Christ shall also raise up your mortal bodies. This place declareth, that the holy Ghost doth belong unto the father, who in the same epistle is showed to belong also unto the son, when as a little before it is said; He that hath not the spirit of Christ, the same is not his. But in the epistle to the Galatians, both together is expressed in these words; And because ye be children, therefore hath God sent the spirit of his son into your hearts, whereby ye cry Abba father. Wherefore, seeing the holy Ghost is the spirit, as well of the father as of the son, he is wholly partaker of their nature.

9. Moreover in the Acts of the Apostles, the fifth chapter, Peter said to Ananias; How darest thou lie unto the Holy Ghost? Thou diddest not lie unto men, but unto God. Now in this place, he most manifestly calleth the Holy Ghost God. Augustine in his book De trinitate, and elsewhere: and Ambrose also De spiritu sancto do both cite the apostle to the Philippians, the third chapter, where he writeth; Beware of dogs, beware of evil workers, beware of concision: for we be the circumcision which serve God in the spirit. Where you see, that the worshiping of God which the Grecians call "λατρεία" (latreia), is done unto the Holy Ghost, which he calleth God. Albeit in some place it is read in the genitive case, "του πνεύματος του Θεού" (tou pneumatos tou Theou): as if thou shouldst say, Serving the spirit of God. I see the place is not very firm; for some interpret it Serving God in spirit: but yet I thought it good to show that the fathers have used this argument. Basil in his treatise De spiritu sancto, the 22nd chap, and also Didymus De spiritu sancto declare that to be God, which can be in diverse places at one time: which thing is not agreeable to any creature. But that the holy Ghost, was present with the apostles and prophets in sundry parts of the world, at one time, no man professing the faith of Christ doubteth: wherefor it followeth that he is God.

Also Basil against Eunomius alleged the epistle of John, the fourth chapter; And in this we know that Christ dwelleth in us, and we in him, because we have received of his spirit: which should not be true, if we should account the holy Ghost to be of another nature than Christ is; for then might the holy Ghost be communicated unto the faithful without Christ. He addeth also another reason; By the holy Ghost we are adopted to be the children of God: wherefore he himself is God. For the scriptures do everywhere call him The spirit of adoption. But none that is not God, can adopt any to be the children of God. In the Acts of the apostles we read; The holy Ghost said, Separate me Paul and Barnabas unto the work of the ministry, whereunto I have chosen them. And there is no doubt, but that it is the part of God only to call unto the ministry. Which reason Athanasius useth in disputing against Arius. There is also brought the twenty chapter of the Acts, where Paul thus admonisheth; Take heed unto the whole flock, wherein the holy Ghost hath made you overseers, to govern the church. But it is the office of none but of God only, to choose ministers and bishops of the churches.

Ambrose thoroughly weigheth of these words; All things are made by him, and he saith, that the holy Ghost spake in the Evangelist: and that therefore if it had been a creature, he should have said; All we things are made by him: by that means he had not excluded himself from the number of creatures. Again, he citeth that saying of John; He shall receive of mine: we cannot (saith he) understand this to be spoken of the body, no nor yet of the soul; and then it must be understood of the divine nature. He also taketh the testimony of Isaiah, which is written in Luke; The Spirit of the Lord hath anointed me, and sent me to preach glad tidings to the poor. But there is none that hath power to send Christ, no not as touching his human nature, unless it be God. We read in the psalm; I will hear what the Lord God will speak in me: but when David spake these words, there was none spake in him but the holy Ghost, wherefore he is God. In the tenth chapter to the Hebrews; The holy Ghost hath testified, This is my testament that I will make unto them: he calleth it his testament, which only God made with his people; wherefore it is manifest that the holy Ghost, which did speak, is God.

10. And in the first epistle of John, the fifth chapter; There be three, which bear witness in heaven, the Father, the Word, and the Spirit; and

these three be one. Many write, that this testimony is not found in the Greek; against whom is Jerome in his preface of the canonical epistles, who saith that these words are in the Greek, but have been left out by the Latin translators. Yet Cyrillus herein agreeth not with Jerome: for he reciteth in the 14th book of his Thesaurus, all this whole place, and omitteth this particle. Among the Latins Augustine and Beda read not these words. But Erasmus in his notes upon this place showeth, that there was found a Greek book in Britain, which had these words: also the Spanish edition hath them. But admit that these words be not had in the Greek copies, the strength of the argument shall not be anything diminished for that cause: for that which we affirm is proved by the other particle of the sentence, which is found extant as well among the Greeks, as among the Latins, namely; There be three things, which bear witness on the earth; blood, water, and the spirit. Augustine against Maximus the Arian bishop, in his third book, the 14th chapter useth this place; and he would, that the spirit should signify the Father, because God is a spirit; and the Father himself is the fountain and beginning of the whole divinity. Further, blood (as he saith) betokens the Son; because he took upon him the nature of man, and shed his blood for us. Finally water, in his judgment, doth manifestly declare the holy Ghost.

Whereunto the Gospel doth very well agree. For whereas Jesus said; Rivers of lively water shall flow out of his belly, it is expounded that he spake this as touching the Spirit, which they should receive that believed in him. Wherefore insomuch as the three persons are represented in these three names, and that it is added withal, that these three be one; it is manifestly declared, that the three divine persons have one and the self-same substance. And Augustine treating upon this place, doth specially urge that particle; And they three be one. And he would have it to be a steadfast and firm thing in the scriptures, that when any things are said to be one, they differ not in substance. Even as when we read in the Gospel, that Christ said; I and the Father be one, there was meant to be one nature, both of the Father, and of the Son: so (saith he) we must now understand as touching these three, that they be one.

11. Cyrillus thus argueth unto this matter: John saith; It is the Spirit which beareth record, and the Spirit is verity, because there be three which bear record upon the earth; The Father, the Word, and the Spirit, and these three are one: but and if ye receive the testimony of men, the testimony of God is greater. In this place thou seest (saith he) that the testimony of the holy Ghost, is called the testimony of God; whereby it is proved, that the holy Ghost is God. And that those three (I mean the spirit, blood, and water) do represent the three persons, it is showed by three reasons. [1] The first is taken from the Analogy or conveniency of the signs: which Augustine recited. [2] Secondly thou perceivest, that those three are said to be one; which is not meet for them, unless thou shalt respect those things which be represented: for otherwise, spirit, blood, and water do vary in nature or kind one from another. [3] Thirdly, those three nouns in the Greek "τὸ ὕδωρ, τὸ πνεῦμα, καὶ τὸ αἷμα" (to hydor, to pneuma, kai to haima), that is water, spirit, and blood be of the neuter gender: unto which afterward is put the masculine article, in the plural number; namely, "οἱ τρεῖς εἰς τὸ ἕν εἰσιν" (hoi treis eis to hen eisin), that is, These three be unto one, or be one. But the masculine article, as touching signs, which be of the neuter gender, might take no place, unless it should be applied unto those which are signified; that is, unto the Father, the Son, and the holy Ghost. Neither let it trouble us, that it is read some-where; These three be unto one, as though it should make for the Arians, which said, that these three persons be unto one, because they consented together in one testimony; as though the speech concerneth not one manner of nature, but one manner of will. And the

phrase cometh near unto the Hebrew: so as To be unto one, and To be one, is the self-same thing. As when we read in the psalm; I will be unto him a Father, and he shall be unto me a Son: it is as if it were said; I will be his Father, and he shall be my Son. And in another place; They shall be unto me a people, and I will be unto them a God, is all one, as to say; I will be their God, and they shall be my people. And when it is said; They be one, there is signified both a distinction of persons, and a unity of substance. For unless there were some distinction, it should have been said; It is one.

12. Also, they allege the song of the three children, wherein, when all creatures are stirred up unto the praises of God, the Son and the holy Ghost are not mentioned: whereby it is plain, that they be not reckoned among creatures. Neither mayest thou say, that this song is a part of the Apocrypha, because this part of Daniel is wanting in the Chaldean edition: for thou shalt see the very same to be done every-where in the Psalms of David, wherein is the same stirring up of creatures unto divine praises. John in his first epistle saith; The spirit is truth: and this cannot be written of a creature, seeing truth is chief and principal, and dependeth not of another. They are wont to allege the beginning of the book of Genesis, where it is said; The spirit of the Lord moved upon the face of the waters. In which place they affirm, that there is mention made of three persons, namely, of the Father, which created; of the Son, by whom all things were made (as when it is said, In the beginning, it is all one, as to say, By the beginning;) and of the holy Ghost. I know that the Hebrew expositors interpret far otherwise of these words; but I have only taken upon me to show those places, by which the fathers gathered the Godhead of the holy Ghost. Whereunto add, that Paul in his epistles seldom maketh mention of the father and the son, but he also speaketh of the holy ghost, either expressly, or by adding of somewhat pertaining

to him. And Basil showeth, that it was a custom received in the whole church, to add in the end of the Psalms, that which we now use; Glory be to the Father, to the Son, and to the holy Ghost, wherein the three persons are made equal the one to the other.

13. The Synod of Nice set forth a creed, in which we say; I believe in the holy Ghost. But it is very manifest, that we must not repose our confidence in anything that is created. And because in those days the contention was not much sprung up of the holy Ghost, there was nothing else added: but afterwards, when diverse and sundry heresies grew up as touching him, then in the Council of Constantinople, which was the second among the four principal, many things were added to make this article plain. For we grant, that We believe in the holy Ghost, both the Lord and giver of life. By the particle (Lord) they make him equal unto Christ, who in the scriptures is commonly called Lord, which epitheton or addition, they would therefore to be expressed, because the Arians affirmed, that Christ was altogether a creature, but yet the noblest (they said) which next unto God was the chief. And they said, that the holy ghost was yet less than the son, and even his minister. Wherefore the Synod in place of Minister, put the title of Lord. The self-same thing did they in the particle; The giver of life: for they saw that it is written in John, that not only the father doth give life, but that the son also can quicken whomsoever he will; and so, least the holy ghost might seem to be excluded from this property, they added that particle. And that his Godhead might be the more manifest, it was added, that He together with the father and the son is worshipped and glorified.

14. Further, Athanasius hath in his creed; God the Father, God the Son, and God the holy Ghost. And to prove this thing, no less is the forgiving of sins taken for an argument which they grant as proper to the holy Ghost. For when Christ had breathed upon his disciples,

he said; Receive ye the holy Ghost, and whose sins ye remit, they be remitted unto them; and whose sins ye retain, they be retained. Whereby it appeareth, that this power is yielded to the holy Ghost, and is proper unto God. And this, even the Scribes themselves testified, who hearing Christ say to the man sick of the palsy; Thy sins be forgiven thee, cried out that he spake blasphemy, in that he durst take upon him the office of God. Furthermore, the holy scriptures do call this self-same spirit, both A sanctifier and giver of light, which faculties are meet to be attributed unto God only. In Exodus, the fourth chapter, it is said unto Moses (when he detracted the time of doing his message, because he had an impediment in his speech;) Who hath given a mouth unto man? Or who maketh the dumb or deaf, the blind and seeing? Have not I the Lord? Wherefore I will be in thy mouth. By which place it is showed, that it is the work of almighty God, to speak in his ministers, to open their mouths, and to make them ready of speech. But Christ, when he speaketh of this matter, saith; It is not you that speak, but the spirit of your father: whereby it seems to be proved, that the holy Ghost is God, seeing he hath one and the self-same action with him.

Augustine in his epistle to Pascentius saith, that he doth wonder how it can be, that Christ, whose members we are, is believed to be God; and that the holy Ghost, whose temple we be, should be denied to be God; seeing the excellency of the Godhead is more proved in the latter condition, than in the first. The reasons which we have brought, do in part prove of necessity, and do plainly show, that the holy Ghost is God. Others indeed be not altogether of such efficacy, but being joined with other things, do confirm the minds of the faithful in this truth; neither is there any of them, which the fathers have not some-where used. There might also be added other arguments of this sort, but with these we will hold ourselves contented.

15. Now remaineth to consider, what is wont to be objected against this doctrine. Some say; The holy Ghost prayeth for us, and that with sighing's unspeakable. How can he then be God, seeing it is not meet for God, to humble himself after the manner of suppliants? Some answer and say; That the son doth make intercession for us, who nevertheless is God, and that therefore to pray, is not strange from the nature of God; howbeit, this is frivolous, For Christ, in that he was man, was inferior to the father, and therefore might be a suitor unto him. But the holy Ghost hath not taken upon him the nature of any creature, into unity of person. Wherefore the respect that must be had towards him, and towards Christ, is far differing and unlike: and therefore we will answer, that the spirit prayeth, and maketh request for us, as it is written in the epistle to the Romans, because it driveth us forward to do these things: and it is therefore said to sigh, because it maketh us to sigh. Neither is this phrase strange from the scriptures, but it is very often used. For God said unto Abraham, when he would have sacrificed his son; Now have I known that thou fearest God. That undoubtedly was known before unto the divine majesty, and was commanded. For the hearts and cogitations of men are not hidden from him. But, I have known, in that place, is as much to say, as, I have caused to know. That this phrase is so to be understood, the Apostle testifieth to the Galatians, when he saith; And seeing ye be children, therefore God hath sent the spirit of his son into your hearts, crying Abba father. In which words he seemeth to affirm, that the holy Ghost himself doth cry unto God. But to the Romans, the same Apostle doth make it very plain; For ye have not received the spirit of bondage, to fear anymore, but ye have received the spirit of adoption of children, whereby we cry Abba father: in which place it appeareth most plainly, that it is we which cry, the holy Ghost stirring and driving us forward thereunto.

16. Further they demand, that If the spirit proceed from the father, and also from the son, what is the cause why he is not called a son, seeing he hath not beginning of himself? We answer; Because that in divine and secret things, we follow both the doctrine and manner of speech of the holy scriptures. Seeing then that the scripture hath in no place said, that the holy Ghost either is begotten, or is the son, why should we attempt thus to say? And doubtless unto godly men this answer should suffice. It must be added moreover, that this issuing out of the holy Ghost, is called a proceeding, therefore we must call it so. And albeit that between the Greek and Latin churches, there was a long contention, whether the holy Ghost proceeded from the son, yet was it not of any great importance, unless it had been aggravated with the spirit of ambition. For after the time that the Grecians began to contend in the Church for primacy, they easily took in ill part the opinions of the Latins. But the dissention was taken up in the Council of Florence, where it was manifest, that the Latins meant no other thing, but that the holy Ghost had his proceeding or issuing out, as well from the father as from the son. The which seeing it may be found, as we have said, that in the holy scriptures it is called a proceeding, we are not to be blamed. The son is said to send the holy Ghost, for when he breathed upon the Apostles, he said; Receive ye the holy Ghost. Again he said; He shall receive of mine. And many of the fathers, before the Council of Florence, wrote, that the holy Ghost is derived as well from the father as the son. Augustine against the heretic Maximinus, and elsewhere, showeth it very plainly. Also Epiphanius in Ancorato confesseth, that the holy Ghost proceedeth from both, that is, from the father and the son.

17. Albeit that between proceeding and generation it is hard to put a difference, and that Augustine in the place now alleged, granteth, that he perceived not the difference: yet he said, that this he knew; namely,

that whatsoever thing groweth, doth also proceed: but he saith not on the other side, that whatsoever things proceed, are also sprung forth. Howbeit, we cannot properly express the difference. Wherefore the holy Ghost is not said, either to be begotten, or unbegotten, least by saying unbegotten, we might seem to affirm him to be the father; or by affirming him to be begotten, we may seem to call him the son. This we have out of Augustine in his third tome, at the beginning of the small questions gathered out of the book De trinitate. Add withal, that if the holy Ghost should be said to be begotten, then in the trinity we should appoint two sons, and two fathers. For, seeing the holy Ghost is as well of the father, as of the son, he should have them both to be his fathers, if it might be said that he is begotten of them: yea, and if the matter be well considered, he might (I say) be called both the son and sons son of one and the self-same Father. For in affirming him to be begotten of the Father, he should be called his Son; but in as much as it should be said, that he is borne of the Son, he should be nephew unto the Father: which things be absurd, and wholly strange from the scriptures. Yea and further, to say that the holy Ghost is begotten, the words of the scripture are against it, which very often do call the Son, The only begotten: whereof it followeth, that the holy Ghost is not begotten.

In the first chapter of John, it is said; We saw the glory thereof, as the glory of the only begotten of the father. And in the third chapter of the same gospel; So God loved the world, as he gave his only begotten son. And the same John in his epistle; In this the love of God towards us appeared, that he gave his only begotten son. And Christ as touching his human nature, hath been accustomed in the scripture to be called, not The only begotten of God, but The first borne among many brethren: as it appeareth in the epistle to the Romans. Howbeit doubtless as touching his divine nature he hath no brethren. There be some which cavil, that in the Synod of Nice, the holy Ghost was not in express words called God; but that only the Godhead of the son was expressed. Unto which objection Epiphanius answereth, that in the Synod of Nice the controversy was as touching the son only. For Arius at the first contended only against this point. And Councils for the most part define not any other things, but such as are called in question: yet nevertheless, if a man diligently examine the matter, he shall see that those things be there defined, which do plainly enough declare the divine nature of the holy Ghost. For it is there said; We believe in the holy Ghost: and it is not lawful for one to put his confidence in a creature. Moreover, that which was doon in the Synod of Nice, was performed in the Synod of Constantinople.

18. Also they object, that among the fathers there were some, and especially of the more ancient of them, which were slack in their writings, to express in plain words the holy Ghost to be God. Among whom Erasmus reckoneth Hilary, who was thought to be the first among the Latins that wrote against the Arians. This father, in his book De trinitate, never by express words called the holy Ghost God. Unto this objection we answer, that the most ancient fathers, in teaching divine things used a singular modesty, and did imitate the holy scriptures so much as they could: and although they said not in express words, that the holy Ghost is God; yet in the mean time they wrote those things, which manifestly prove his Godhead. And further it appeareth, that they of set purpose disputed against them, which denied the Godhead of the holy Ghost, and equality of the three divine persons: as we see by the strife that was about the word Homousion; from which many of the Catholics at the beginning did restrain themselves, because it seemed to be but new, and that it was not had in the holy scriptures: and yet they nevertheless did embrace and most willingly admit the thing signified. Howbeit we strive not about these things, but grant first and chiefly whatsoever is in the

holy scriptures: and then whatsoever is necessarily and manifestly derived out of them. Next unto those ancienter sort of fathers did Basil, and diverse others succeed; which by all means both testify and defend the holy Ghost to be God.

19. Others cavil, because it is written; that None knoweth the Father but the Son, and on the other side; None the Son, but the Father: in which places they say, that there is no mention of the holy Ghost; and therefore it seemeth unto them, that he knoweth neither the Father, nor yet the Son, and that for the same cause he is not God. To these also we answer, that when the knowing of the Father, and of the Son is attributed to two persons, the holy Ghost must not be excluded; seeing he is said to be the spirit as well of the Father as of the Son: wherefore that which is belonging to both, is also common unto him. And if they demand a plain testimony hereof out of the scriptures, we will bring forth one out of the first epistle to the Corinth. where it is written; The things of man none knoweth, but the spirit of man, which is within him: and even so those things which be of God, none knoweth but the spirit of God. Also it is written in the gospel; Blessed art thou Simon the son of Jonah: for flesh and blood hath not revealed these things unto thee, but the spirit of my father, which is in heaven. By these testimonies it is manifest, that the holy Ghost doth not only know God, but doth also reveal and make him to be known unto others.

But this error, whereby some endeavor, to rebuke the holy Ghost with an ignorance of heavenly things, took beginning from Origin, who affirmed a certain degree to be among the natures of Intelligences; so as he though that the Father knoweth himself only; and he said that the Son did not know the Father; and that the holy Ghost knew not the Son: and he would moreover, that the angels perceive not the holy Ghost, and lastly that men see not the angels. And that this order is set down by him, Epiphanius showeth out of the book, as he testifieth, <H&G>; in which book nevertheless, so far as hitherto I remember, I have not read the matter plainly in such sort described. Which is no marvel; for that book which Ruffinus translated, hath many things imperfect. For he plucked out those things, which he thought tended most unto error, least the readers should be too much offended, whereby afterward there arose a great discord between him and Jerome.

20. There were some which affirmed, that seeing the holy Ghost is said to be sent, in like manner as the Son is said to be sent; he should have taken upon him, even as Christ did, some visible nature into the unity of person: which reason of theirs is not necessary. We grant, that sometimes he took upon him either a dove, or fiery tongues, by which he declared his presence; howbeit, these he took but for a time: neither was he made one person with these two natures, as we grant it to have come to pass in Christ. Albeit there have been most impudent heretics, as Manes, of whom the Manichees were named; as were Montanus, Basilides, and such other pestilent men, which published themselves to be the holy Ghost, whom Christ had promised. But in vain were these things devised by them; for the Acts of the Apostles do sufficiently declare, that the promise of Christ was performed within a few days after his ascension.

21. But it must be considered, that the scripture speaketh of God after the manner of men, for the affect of remembrance declareth the goodness of God: for they which be mindful of their friends in danger, do (for the most part) relieve them. Howbeit, to remember, accordeth not properly with God, seeing it noteth a certain forgetfulness that went before; which to ascribe unto God, were an unjust thing. But of knowing's we see there be three kinds, the which are distinguished one from another, according to the difference of time. For if a thing present he found out, to one which then beholdeth, it is called a certain beholding:

and this knowledge is the root of all the other, and more surer than the rest. Further, if it have respect unto things that be past, it is called memory. If unto things to come, it is foresight; which third (for the most part) springeth from the second. For they which have experience of many things, and remember much, are wont by a certain wisdom achieved, to have great judgment of things to come. Of these kinds of knowledge, none is truly attributed unto God, but the first, seeing all things are present with him: and even as his nature, so his actions are by no means comprehended within the course of time. But yet it is said in the scriptures, that either he remembered, or that he foresaw; because oftentimes those effects are attributed unto him, which they are wont to do that foresee or remember anything. But memory requireth a knowledge that is past. We shall find that the scripture hath said, that Noah was just and perfect in his generations. Then when he was minded to save him, and had made him safe in the ark, he seemed to attend for him: and when he had tarried so long shut up in the ark, and was not delivered from thence (if I shall speak after the manner of men) God seemed in a manner to forget him. And again, when he delivereth him, he is said to remember.

22. So, when it is said, that God waxed angry, it is not so to be understood, as though God were troubled with affects; for that belongeth unto men: but according to the common and received exposition of these places, we understand it, that God behaved himself like unto men that be angry. After the self-same manner it is sometimes written, that he repented him: wherefore God, either to repent, or to be angry, is nothing else, but that he doth those things, which men repenting, or being angry, are wont to do. For the one sort do either alter or undo all that ever they had done before; and the other revenge themselves of such wrongs as have been done unto them. Ambrose in his book of

Noah and the ark, the fourth chapter, speaketh otherwise of the anger of God. For neither (saith he) doth God think as men do, as though he should be of any new mind; neither is he angry, as though he were mutable. But these things are therefore believed, to the intent that the bitterness of our sins may be expressed, which hath deserved the wrath of God, that so much, and so far forth hath the fault increased, as even God (which naturally is not moved, either with anger, hatred, or any other passion) may seem to be provoked unto wrath. And rightly is there mention made of anger, before that punishment is rehearsed; for men use first to be angry, before they revenge. And anger (if we may believe Aristotle in his Rhetoric's) is nothing else, but a desire of revengement, because of contempt. For they that perceive themselves to be despised and contemned, do straightway think upon revenge, and do continually meditate how they may, by means of some punishment, requite either the injury or contumely that is done.

23. But yet peradventure some man will doubt, whether God, when he repented him, were in any respect changed. All the godly in a manner with one mouth confess, that God cannot be changed one jot, because that would be a certain sign, both of imperfection, and also of inconstancy: but they say, that this variety which happeneth herein, must not be ascribed to God himself, but unto us. For example sake. If one will say, that God out of all doubt ceased to favor the Chananits, against the children of Israel, whom he before so seemed to strengthen, as he would have them to oppress the Jews: and again, that he afterward exalted the Hebrews, whom before it seemed that he would have to be kept under by the Chananits; certainly no man can deny, but that these things be true. How shall we therefore defend, that the will of God is without alteration. I answer out of Jeremiah the 18th chapter, that undoubtedly there appeareth a plain diversity to be in the effects, whereas God

notwithstanding doth always retain one manner of will. For thus it is there written in his name; So soon as I shall speak against a kingdom or nation, to destroy it, root it out, and overthrow it, if they shall repent, I also will repent. And contrariwise, when I shall speak good of a kingdom or people, to set them up and plant them; and that nation or kingdom shall do evil in my sight, I also will repent of the good which I meant to do unto them. These words show, that God is not variable in these kind of promises and threatening's; for he speaketh not absolutely and simply, but upon condition. But the fulfilling, or making void of the conditions, is looked for in us: wherefore the change must not be attributed unto him, but unto us.

But if thou wilt ask me, whether God hath known and decreed before what shall come to pass, as touching these conditions; I will grant he hath. For even at the first beginning, he not only knew what the events of things would be, but also decreed what should be. But seeing the secretness of his will, touching these things, is not opened unto us in the holy scriptures; therefore we must follow that rule, which is given by Jeremiah, even as we have rehearsed before. This rule, the Ninevites, and also Hezekiah the king had respect unto, even before the same was published. For although that destruction was denounced to them in the name of God, yet they escaped from it; by reason of the repentance and prayers, which they in the meantime used. Neither is there any cause why we should suspect that God doth lie in anything, when he threateneth or promiseth those things which do not afterward come to pass. For as touching Hezekiah, death was undoubtedly to have taken hold of him, by reason of natural causes, commonly called the second causes: wherefore the sentence being pronounced according to those causes, he might not be accused of a lie. Also the Ninevites (if God had done by them as their sins deserved) there had been no other way with them but destruction. And God commanded Jonah to preach unto them, according to their deserts. Furthermore a lie, which in talk hath a supposition or condition joined therewith, cannot be blamed in such sort, as it may be in arguments which he absolute and without exception: seeing the event dependeth of the performing or violating of the condition.

CHAPTER TWO

OF THE CREATION OF ALL THINGS

I would think that under the name of heaven and earth, Moses showed that the foundation or ground of all things, as well of the heavens, as of the elements was made, and that this matter is signified by the names of things already finished. For seeing it cannot be known otherwise, but by the form and perfection, it is meet that that also should be named and specified. Wherefore this whole heap is signified by the name of heaven and earth; wherein also come the other three elements, fire, air, and water. He showed us of the uttermost things, by which he will also have us to know the things that are between both. But how far these things at the first were out of square and order it is showed, when of the earth it is said; It was without form, and waste. Wherefore this rude heap was brought forth, being as yet, stuff or matter void of order, the which belonged as well to the upper things, as to the lower. And so perhaps, as the more noble had the uppermost place; so to the less noble was assigned the nethermost: for this cause, the name of creation is very fit for the first and unorderly heap. For those things seem only to be made of nothing, and other things are said to be made and fashioned. And yet this difference is not observed in all things; for some things are called created, which are said to be derived from some former matter. Two things doubtless men have been accustomed to attribute unto creation, both that it should be of a sudden, and that it require no matter to be beforehand.

2. Thus the world was not rashly made, neither is it coeternal with the maker or creator. Many of the ancient philosophers assigned the workmanship of things unto rashness and chance; seeing diverse of them in the stead of beginnings, named discord and debate, or else such little small bodies, as smaller cannot be. Aristotle attributed eternity unto that, whereby he maketh God, not to be the working cause of the world; but only attributed unto him the cause of the end: or if he do, he taketh from him the power of working according to his will; and thinketh that the world followeth him, as a shadow doth the body, or as the light doth the sun. Which the Peripatetikes will seem to do for divine honor sake, least they should be driven to ascribe any lack of power or alteration in God. But these things hurt not us at all; for we affirm not, that God is borne, or apt to suffer anything: but we attribute unto him the chiefest power to do. And although God in his eternity, minded to make the world, it followeth not therefore, that when he did make it, there was in him any alteration of his purpose or will. Again, let us beware of the error of them in old time, which thought that there was an eternal and uncreated Chaos, or confused heap, extant before: and that God did only pick out those things, which were there mingled together. But we say, that the same heap also was made the first day. Some there be which demand, that seeing God could have brought forth the world

long before, why he did it so late? This is an arrogant and malapert question, wherein man's curiosity cannot be satisfied; but by beating down the folly thereof. For if I should grant thee, that the world was made before, at any certain instant of time, that thou couldest imagine; yet thou mightest still complain, that the same was but lately made, if thou refer thy cogitation to the eternity of God: so as we must herein deal after a godly manner, and not with this malapert and rash curiosity.

Of Angels and their creation.

3. But verily it seems to be a marvel, why the creation of Angels is so kept in silence, as there is no mention thereof in all the Old Testament: in the Old Testament (I say) because in the New Testament it is spoken of. In the first chapter to the Colossians, there is plain mention of their creation. There be some, which bring two places of the Old Testament, namely; Who maketh his Angels spirits. And in another place, when he said; And they be made. Howbeit these places do not firmly persuade it. It should be rather said, that they are comprehended under the name of heaven, seeing it is generally received, that the heavens are turned about by them. The first reason is, because if their creation had been first described, it might have seemed, that God used their labor in the bringing forth of other things. But to the intent we should attribute unto God the whole power of creation, therefore did Moses keep it in silence; least perhaps we might suspect ourselves to be their workmanship. And even as our redemption is only attributed unto Christ the son of God, and not to the Angels; so was it meet to be as touching our creation. The second reason; because of the proneness of men unto idolatry: for if they have worshipped heaven, stars, four-footed beasts, serpents, and birds; what would they have done, if Moses had described that spiritual creature in his colors; and had said, that they were made to do us service, to be presidents over countries, and to be at hand with every man?

What would not men have done? They would have run a madding to the worshipping of them. The first mention of them was at paradise with the sword of the cherubim's. Also in Abraham's time, when there was present an exceeding strong deliverer. For even then are dangers permitted by God, when most strong remedies are also used by him. And as touching this superstitious worshipping of Angels, Paul speaketh in the second to the Colossians.

4. Rabbi Selomoh saith that the names of Angels are secret; so as they, even themselves, do not know their own names: yea, and he addeth, that they have not names of their own, but that only surnames are appointed them of those things, unto which they are sent to take charge of. Whereunto the epistle to the Hebrews assenteth, when it calleth them Administering spirits. Rabbi Selomoh bringeth examples out of the holy scriptures. An Angel was sent unto Isaiah, and because he put unto his lips a burning coal, he was called Seraphim, of the Hebrew verb Saraph, which signifieth To burn. So of Raphael we may say, that he which cured Tobias was so called; as who should say; He was the medicine of God. And Gabriel, by the same reason is called The strength of God. Also the word Peli, which the Angel attributed to himself in the 13th of Judges, signifieth Wonderful: for he came, to the intent he might do a miracle. And surly it was very wonderful, to bring out a flame out of a rock, which consumed the sacrifice. And it may be, that the Angel would not open his name; because men in those days were prone unto idolatry: and perhaps, when they had heard the name of the Angel, they would soon have been induced to worship it, more than right religion requireth. But Cherubim be Angels, whose name is derived of a figure. Ibn-ezra saith, that Keruf signifieth, A form or figure, be it either of man, or of brute beasts, it maketh no matter which, seeing either of both is so called. Angels have these names, because they appear unto men, in figure or

form of a living creature, as it appeareth in the tenth of Ezekiel. Others think, that the name is compounded of the Hebrew letter <H&G>, which is a mark of similitude; and of Raui, which in the Chaldean speech signifieth Boys, or Young men, because Angels appeared in the form of men, and that of young men. And to that similitude those in the tabernacle were made, having wings put to them. Which peradventure Dionysius, and other followed; when they say, that they are signified by the fullness of knowledge, seeing a man, whose figure they bear, differeth in understanding and knowledge from brute beasts.

Wherefore Cherub is a certain figure given, and betokeneth unto us The messengers of God, which with great celerity do all those things which God commandeth. He useth them, and rideth as it were upon the winds, which are governed by those Angels, because by those things, that which God would, is brought to pass. Also, the Ethnics made Mercury with wings, and attributed wings unto the winds. The Angels likewise are often-times put with wings. In Exodus, the Cherubim are made with wings. Isaiah saith, that Seraphim came flying unto him. Ezekiel and Daniel saw Angels flying unto them. These things declare, that the ministry of Angels is exceeding swift. In the 104th Psalm; Who maketh his Angels spirits. We must not here imagine with the Sadducees, as though the Angels were but a bare service of no substance, severed from matter. They are not only moved with the moving that brute creatures have, but they understand, they speak, and they instruct us. An Angel came unto the virgin Marie, and unto Zechariah. Their Angels (as it is in the Gospel) do always behold the face of their heavenly father. Unto the Hebrews they are called Administering spirits. Finally, they govern kingdoms and provinces.

5. It followeth, that I speak somewhat of the visions of Angels. For an Angel appeared unto Manoah; and oftentimes in other places, as

the scriptures declare, Angels have been seen of men. But it may be demanded, how they did appear, whether with any body, or only in fantasy: and if with a body, whether with their own body, or with a strange body: and whether the body were taken for a time, or forever? Of these things, there be diverse opinions of men. The Platonists say, that The minds, that is, the Intelligences are so framed, that certain of them have celestial bodies, and some have fiery bodies, some airy, some watery, and some earthy bodies, and some they affirm to be dark spirits, which do continually dwell in darkness and mist. Of these things Marsilius Ficinus hath gathered many things, in his tenth book De legibus, and in his Argument of Epinomis. The Peripatetikes affirm, that there be certain Intelligences, which guide and turn about the celestial circles, neither make they mention of any other. Also the school divines have decreed, that those minds and Intelligences are altogether spiritual, and that they have no bodies. And they were led thus to think, by reason that these Intelligences must needs excel the souls of men, whose perfectest faculty consisteth in understanding. Wherefore (as they think) it is meet, that in this work, the Intelligences should much exceed them: and that this cometh to pass, because those heavenly minds have no need of images or of senses, the which being so, it should be superfluous for them to have bodies.

6. But among the Fathers, some have affirmed far otherwise. Origin in his books <H&G> (as Jerome hath noted in his epistle Ad Pammachium de erroribus Johannes Hierosolymitani) saith, that Those spiritual minds, so often as they offend, do fall, and are thrust into bodies, but yet not immediately into the vilest bodies; but first into starry bodies, then into fiery and airy, afterward into watery, and last of all into human and earthy bodies: and if then also they behave not themselves well, they become devils. And further, that if they will yet then repent, they may

come again by the self-same degrees unto their former state. And this he saith, we should understand by that ladder, upon which Jacob saw the Angels ascending and descending. But Jerome, to make the matter more plain, giveth a similitude. If a tribune (saith he) do not rightly execute his office, he is put from that degree, and is made a principal secretary, afterward a senator, a captain over two hundredth, a ruler over fewer, a constable of a watch, afterward a man at arms, and after that, a soldier of the meanest degree. And although a tribune were once a common soldier, yet of a tribune he is not made a young soldier, but a principal secretary. Howbeit, these things be absurd, and worthy to be laughed at. And certainly herein Origin speaketh more like a Platonist, than a Christian. That which he first affirmeth; namely, that souls are thrust into bodies, as unto punishments, is manifestly false; forsomuch as God hath joined the body to the soul, for a help, not for a punishment. Neither doth he well, to put the devil into any hope of salvation in time to come, seeing Christ hath taught the contrary, saying; Go ye cursed into eternal fire, prepared for the devil and his angels. Neither can we in that place understand Eternal, to be only a long space of time. For Christ most plainly expoundeth his meaning, when he saith; Their worm shall not die, and their fire shall not be quenched. Neither did he truly affirm, that the souls first sinned, before they came into bodies; seeing Paul writeth of Jacob and Esau, that before they were borne, and had doon neither good nor evil, it was said; Jacob have I loved, and Esau have I hated: the greater shall serve the lesser. Upon just cause therefore is this opinion of Origin rejected by all men.

7. Augustine in many places seemeth to attribute bodies unto Angels; and namely in his second book De trinitate, the seventh chapter, and in the third book, the first chapter. Which the school men perceiving, excused him, saying, that he spake not there after his own judgment, but

according to the judgment of others. Which thing I also might allow, for so much as I see, that that father in his eight book and 16th chapter De civitate Dei, (after the opinion of Apuleius Madaurensis and Porphyrius) defineth, that Angels be in kind, sensible creatures; in soul, passive; in mind, reasonable; in body, airy; in time, eternal. Doubtless herein he followeth the doctrine of the Platonists; but in the places before alleged, he seemeth to speak altogether of himself. Yea and Barnard also, upon the song of the three children (as it appeareth) is of the same opinion. Wherefore the schoolmen be compelled to devise another shift, and they say; that Angels, if they be compared with men, are spirits: but if with God, they have bodies, because they are destitute of the single and pure nature of God. Tertullian De carne Christi affirmeth, that Angels have bodies: but that is the less marvel in him; for he attributeth a body even to God himself. But he calleth a body, whatsoever is; for he dealt with unlearned and rude men, which think, that whatsoever is not a body, is nothing. But the schoolmen say, that Angels in very deed are spirits; but that when they come unto men, they take upon them airy bodies, which they thicken and make very gross, whereby they can both be seen, touched, and perceived, beyond the nature of air. There be some also, which say, that some earthy or waterish thing is mixed with them; but in no wise will grant the same to be any perfect mixture, least they should be compelled there to appoint a generation. There have been also which thought, that Angels took upon them dead carcasses: but this to the more part seemeth an unworthy thing, to be thought of the holy Angels.

8. Here will some man say, that it is an absurd thing to charge the celestial Angels with feigning and lying; as they to feign themselves to be men, and yet are none indeed. Yea and this seemeth to weaken the argument of Christ, which he used after his resurrection, to declare that he had a very body indeed; Feel (saith he) and see: for a spirit hath no

flesh and bones, as ye see me have. For the apostles, being dismayed, thought that they had seen a spirit; and therefore to bring them out of doubt, Christ bad them to handle and feel his body. But the apostles might have said; That which we feel is a fantasy, it seemeth indeed to be Christ, but perhaps it is not. For Angels also seem to have bodies, and to be touched and felt, whereas yet they have no bodies indeed. Also this opinion may weaken the argument of the fathers against Marcion, as touching the flesh of Christ. For he did eat (say they) he drank, he was hungry, he slept, he did sweat, and such like; and therefore had a true and human body. Unto these things might be answered, that the self-same things have happened unto Angels, whereas notwithstanding they had no bodies. I answer; that which they first say, that it is absurd to charge the Angels with lies; they should understand that everything, howsoever it be feigned, is not straightway a lie. Christ appeared unto his disciples as a stranger, and yet he lied not; even he was seen unto Marie in likeness of a gardener, yet he lied not: so the Angels, although they appeared to be men, when they were no men, yet were they no liars. For they came not of purpose to prove themselves men, but only that they might converse and have communication with men.

To the argument of Christ, as touching his own body, thus I answer: first, the apostles thought that it had been a ghost, which appeared: and therefore Christ, to refell that, saith; Handle and see, for a spirit hath neither flesh nor bones. By the handling it self it might be perceived, that the same, which was present, was a very true and perfect body, not a vain fantasy. But thou wilt say; It was a true body indeed, but yet taken for a time, and such a body as Angels sometime are wont to put on. But how could it be proved, that it was the same body which lay before in the sepulcher? Herein the authority of Christ, and of the scriptures must be of force: for the scriptures teach plainly enough, that Christ should die, and afterward rise again the third day: but nothing can rise again, except that which fell before, as Tertullian doth very learnedly write. And this did the Schoolmen perceive; whereupon Thomas Aquinas saith, that unless something else can be added, this is no good argument. The same may be answered unto the reasons of the fathers against Marcion. Indeed many of the actions before alleged, may be fit for Angels, or bodies assumed: but yet not all. For, to be borne and nourished, to die and to feel, happen neither unto Angels, nor yet unto bodies assumed. But the scripture doth most plainly testify, that Christ was borne, that he sorrowed, that he was hungry, that he suffered death, and that he was very true man. But of these things more at large hereafter.

9. There be many other things in the school Divines, as touching these matters: but because they are not so profitable, I will omit them, and will demand this; Whether Angels may take very bodies upon them, and those natural, which were bodies before, and may use them at their liberty, as the devil did put on the serpent, and thereby deceived Eve? An Angel also spake in Balaam's asse, wherefore then cannot an Angel after the same manner possess a human body, and speak therein? Doubtless it is written in the prophet Zechariah; The Angel of the Lord, which spake in me. Wherefore it appeareth, that Angels may use the bodies of men and beasts. Augustine in his third book De trinitate, the first chapter saith, that This is a very hard question, whether Angels may adjoin bodies to their own proper bodies, and change them into diverse forms; as we use to do garments, or also to change them into very nature, as we read that Christ did, when he turned water into wine: this he saith is not impossible to be done. For thus he writeth; I confess it passeth the strength of my capacity, whether that Angels, retaining the spiritual quality of their own body, may in working more secretly by it, take to them something of the more gross inferior elements, which being framed

fit to themselves, may alter and turn the same, as it were a garment, into all bodily forms or shapes; yea, even into the true things themselves, as true water was turned into true wine by the Lord: or else, whether they can transform their own proper bodies into what they will, being applied to that thing which they go about to do. But whether of these be true, it belongeth not to the present question. But I say, that if there were very bodies of Angels, then was Christ's argument firm. And I will more willingly grant unto this, than to say as some do, that Angels deceived the senses of men. For after this manner they will strive against us, when we say that in the Eucharist remaineth bread, which is both seen and touched; as they may answer, that indeed it seemeth bread, but yet it is none: even as Angels seemed to be men, when as yet they were no men. Truly I deny not, but that sometimes the senses may be deceived; but yet I affirm, that there be two kinds of those things which are perceived by the sense. For some things are common unto many senses, and others are proper unto someone sense alone. For figure, quantity, and number, are perceived of many senses: and doubtless in such things the senses may be deceived. As Carneades was wont to dispute of bending an ore in the water, and of the bigness of the body of the sun. But in things which properly be sensible, the sense is never deceived, unless it be long of some impediment of the body, or overmuch distance, or some such like let. Wherefore, seeing that in the Eucharist our sense doth show us that bread remaineth, there is no need to feign that the sense is therein deceived.

10. But to appoint a certain compendious way of this disputation, three ways come to mind, by which it may seem that the Angels appeared. [1] For either they were seen in fantasy, so as they were thought to have bodies, when they had not (which way cannot be approved; for they did not beguile the senses, and they were not seen only of one

person, but of many, and at many and sundry times, and were in such sort seen, as Abraham washed some of their feet, and Jacob wrestled a whole night with an Angel:) [2] or else they verily appeared with a true body, which notwithstanding was not such a body, as it was thought to be: [3] or else they had the very self-same body, truly and in very deed, which they seemed to have. Tertullian De carne Christi, hath written most learnedly of this third sort; Thou hast sometimes (saith he) both read and believed, that the Angels of the Creator were turned into the shape of a man, and that they carried such a truth of a body, as both Abraham washed their feet, and Lot by their hands was plucked from the Sodomites. An Angel also wrestled with a man, and desired to be loosed from the weight of the body of him, by whom he was held. That therefore, which was lawful unto Angels, which be inferior unto God (namely, that they being turned into the corpulency of men, and yet nevertheless remained Angels) this dost thou take away from God, which is more mighty: as though Christ, taking true manhood upon him, were not able to remain God? Thus Tertullian disputeth against the Marcionites; for they affirmed, that Christ did seem to have, but yet indeed had not, the body of a man. Tertullian objecteth against them; And if ye grant this (saith he) unto the Angels, that they have had bodies; why do ye not much rather yield the same unto the son of God? And he addeth; Or did these Angels also appear in fantasy of flesh? But thou darest not say so. For if thou account so of the Angels of the Creator, as thou dost of Christ, Christ shall be of the same substance that Angels be of, and the Angels shall be such as Christ is. If thou haddest not of set purpose rejected the scriptures, which are contrary to thy opinion, and corrupted others, the Gospel of John would herein have abashed thee, which declareth, that The spirit coming down in the body of a dove, lighted upon the Lord, which, being the spirit, was as truly a dove, as he was the spirit: neither did the contrary substance taken, destroy his own proper substance.

11. I know there have been some schoolmen, which thought, that it was not a very dove, which descended upon the head of Christ, but that it was only an airy and thickened body, appearing to be a dove. But Augustine De agone Christiano writeth otherwise; namely, that the same was a very dove. For a thing (saith he) is more effectual to express the property of the holy Ghost, than is a sign. Even as Christians also are better expressed in sheep and lambs, than in the likeness of sheep and lambs. Again, if Christ had a true body, and deceived not; then the holy Ghost had the very true body of a dove. Tertullian addeth; Thou wilt demand where the body of the dove became, when the spirit was taken again into heaven, and in like manner of the Angels bodies? It was taken away, even after the self-same manner that it came. If thou haddest seen when it was brought forth of nothing, thou mightest also have known when it was taken away to nothing. If the beginning of it was not visible, no more was the end; then he remitteth the reader unto John: Was he also (saith he) a fantasy after his resurrection, when he offered his hands and feet to be seen of his disciples, saying; Behold, it is I; for a spirit hath not flesh and bones as ye see me have? Therefore Christ is brought in as a juggler or conjurer. And in his third book against Marcion; Therefore his Christ, that he should not lie nor deceive, and by that means perhaps might be esteemed for the Creator, was not indeed that which he seemed to be, and that which he was, he was feigned to be: flesh, and yet no flesh; man, and yet no man, and therefore Christ; God, and not God. For why did he not also bear the shape of God? Shall I believe him as touching this inward substance, that is overthrown about the outward substance? How may he be thought to work soundly in secret, that is perceived to be false openly? And afterward; It is enough for me to affirm that, which is

agreeable unto God, namely, the truth of that thing which he objecteth to three senses, to sight, to touching, and to hearing. Again, in his book De carne Christi, His virtues (saith he) proved that he had the spirit of God; and his passions, that he had the flesh of man. If virtues be not without spirit, neither shall passions be without flesh. If flesh together with the passions be feigned, the spirit also with his virtues is false. Why doest thou make division of Christ by an untruth? He is all wholly truth.

12. Apelles the heretic, being in a manner vanquished with these reasons, agreed indeed that Christ was endued with very flesh, but yet denied the same to be born, but said, that it was brought forth from heaven. And he objecteth, that The bodies which were taken by Angels, were true bodies, but were not borne: such a body (saith he) Christ had. Whereunto Tertullian answereth, They (saith he) which publish the flesh of Christ to be after the example of the Angels, saying, that it was not borne, namely a fleshy substance, I would have them also to compare the causes, as well why Christ, as why the Angels did come in the flesh. For there was never any Angel that came down to be crucified, to suffer death, and to rise again. If then there was never any such cause for Angels to incorporate themselves, then hast thou a cause why they take flesh, and yet were not borne. They came not to die, therefore they came not to be borne; but Christ being sent to die, it was necessary that he should be borne; for no man is wont to die, but he which is borne. He addeth moreover; And even then also the Lord himself, among those Angels, appeared unto Abraham, with flesh indeed, without nativity, by reason of the same diversity of cause. After this he addeth, that Angels have their bodies rather from the earth than from heaven. For let them prove (saith he) that those Angels received of the stars substance of flesh; if they prove it not, because it is not written, then was not the flesh of Christ from thence, whereunto they apply their example. And in his third book

against Marcion; My God (saith he) which having taken it out of the slime of the earth, formed it a new unto this quality, not as yet by the seed of matrimony, and yet flesh notwithstanding, might as well of any matter have framed flesh unto Angels, which also of nothing framed the world, and that with a word, into so many and such bodies.

Again, in his book De carne Christi; it is manifest, that Angels bare not flesh proper of their own, as in the nature of spiritual substance: and if they were of any body, yet was it of their own kind; and for a time they were changeable into human flesh, to the intent they might be seen and converse with men. Further, in the third book against Marcion; Understand thou (saith he) that neither it must be granted thee, that the flesh in Angels was an imagined thing, but of a true and perfect human substance. For if it were not hard for him to give both true senses and acts unto that imagined flesh, much easier was it for him, that he gave a true substance of flesh to true senses and actions: insomuch as he is the very proper author and worker thereof. For it is harder for God to make a lie, than to frame a body. Last of all, he thus concludeth; Therefore are they very human bodies, because of the truth of God, who is far from lying and deceit: and because they cannot be dealt withal by men, after the manner of men, otherwise than in the substance of men. I might allege many other things out of Tertullian, but these may seem to suffice for this present purpose. Briefly, he thinketh that Angels have bodies for a time, but yet strange, and not their own: for their own bodies (as he thinketh) belongeth unto the spiritual kind. Secondly, he saith, that those strange bodies, which they take unto them, are either created of nothing; or else of some such matter, as seemeth best to the wisdom of God. Thirdly he teacheth, that those bodies were true and substantial, and human bodies; not vain or feigned, but of very flesh; and not of that, which only appeared to be flesh: in such wise, as of men, they might both be touched and handled; to the intent that both he might remove dissimulation from God, and also confirm the truth of human flesh in Christ. Whereby it is proved, that men's senses beguiled then not as touching these things; as the Papists confirm, that men are deceived about the bread and wine of the Eucharist.

13. But Origin in his book <H&G>, as Jerome citeth him against John bishop of Jerusalem, was of a far other mind. For whereas we say, that the visions of Angels may be conceived three manner of ways; to wit, either in fantasy, or in body, but not human: or else in the very true body of a man; he taketh a certain mean, and saith; that The bodies of Angels, wherein they present themselves to the eyes of men, are neither perfect bodies, nor human bodies, nor yet fantastical bodies, and yet bodies nevertheless: and that he applieth to them that rise again. For we shall (saith he) have bodies in the resurrection, but yet only bodies, not bones, not sinews, not flesh. And indeed there is some difference between a body and flesh: for every flesh is a body, but everybody is not flesh. Such a difference Paul toucheth in the first chapter of his epistle to the Colossians, when he said; Ye are reconciled in the body of his flesh. And in the second chapter; By putting off the sinful body of the flesh. Yea, and in the Creed also we say; that We believe in the resurrection of the flesh, and say not; Of the body. Origin said, that he saw two exceeding errors; the one was, of them which said, that there was no resurrection. Such were the Valentinians and Marcionites; of which sort also were Hymenaeus and Philetus, who (as Paul witnesseth) taught that the resurrection was already past; and such are the Libertines at this day reported to be. For they babble (I cannot tell what) of the matter both ungodly, and unlearnedly. Another of those which think, that perfect and true bodies shall rise again with flesh, sinews, and bones: which thing

(he saith) is not possible; for Flesh and blood cannot inherit the kingdom of God.

But Origin should have weighed what Paul said afterward: for he addeth; Neither shall corruption possess incorruption. Wherefore, his meaning is, that a corruptible body cannot possess the kingdom of God. But Origin, to keep himself within that mean, which he appointed, confessed that bodies indeed shall rise again, yet not gross and bony, but spiritual: according as Paul said; It shall rise a spiritual body. But Origin in these words marked not, that Paul calleth it A spiritual body; not because it shall be wholly converted into a spirit, but because it shall have spiritual qualities: namely, incorruption, and most clear brightness. But because he perceived, that the body of Christ, which he after his resurrection offered to his disciples to be handled and felt, was against his doctrine, therefore he saith; Let not the body of Christ deceive you, for it had many singular properties, which are not granted unto other bodies. Further, he would have a true body after his resurrection, to the intent he might prove by this dispensation, that he was truly risen from the dead: not to signify that other bodies should be semblable unto it at the resurrection. But he showed the nature of a spiritual body at Emmaus, when he vanished from the sight of his disciples; and at another time, when he went in to his disciples, the doors being fast shut.

14. Against these things Jerome repugneth; If Christ (saith he) after his resurrection, did verily eat with his disciples, he had also a very true body: if he did not eat, how did he by a false thing prove the truth of his body? In that he vanished from the sight of his disciples, this was not through the nature of his body, but by his own power: for so in Nazareth, when the people would have assailed him with stones, he withdrew himself out of their sight. And shall we not think, that the son of God was able to do that, which a magician could do? For Apollonius

Tyanaeus, when he was brought into the council before Domitian, he forthwith vanished away. That this was in Christ, not in respect of the nature of his body, but of his divine power, it is showed by that which went before in the history. For while he was in the way with his disciples, their eyes were held, so as they could not know him. And whereas Origin affirmeth, that the body of Christ was spiritual, because it came in where the doors were shut: Jerome answereth, that the creature gave place to the creator, &c. Wherefore the body of Christ pierced not through the midst of the planks and boards, so as two bodies had been together in one and the self-same place; but herein was the miracle, in that the very timber of the doors gave way unto the body of Christ.

Further, whereas some do object, that the body of Christ came forth of the sepulcher being close shut; that also is not of necessity to be believed: but it may be thought that the stone was rolled away before he came out. And least any should think that I devise this of myself, let him read the 83rd epistle of Leo unto the bishops of Palestine; The flesh (saith he) of Christ which came out of the sepulcher, the stone being rolled away, &c. Now to return to the purpose. Because I said that the bodies of Angels, which they take unto them, may be thought either to have been fantastical or spiritual, or else substantial and very human bodies; and that the two first opinions are rejected: it now resteth, that the bodies of Angels, wherein they show themselves to be men, are very true and human bodies: and this only I affirm to be true, seeing Angels were in such sort seen, as they wrestled with men, and offered their feet to be washed. And I judge it not lawful to say, that men's senses were there deceived, seeing the things were outwardly done. I deny not indeed, but that sometimes there happened to the prophets visions imaginative, when they said that they saw God or the cherubim's, or such other like things. For in as much as that happened often in their mind or power imaginative, it might be done by forms, images, and visions.

15. Now remaineth two things to be examined; one whether the Angels, having in this wise put on human bodies, may be called men. I think not: for if we understand human flesh, which is formed and borne a soul reasonable, surly it cannot be said that Angels in this sort have human flesh. What then (will some say) were the senses beguiled when men saw them? No verily: for the senses do only judge of outward things, and of such things as be apparent: but what doth inwardly force or move those things, which they see, they judge not; this is the part of reason to seek and search out. It must also be added, that Angels did not always keep those bodies with them; because they were not joined unto them in one and the self-same substance, so as the Angel and the body should become one person. The holy Ghost also, although it was a very dove wherein he descended, yet was not he together of one substance with it; wherefore the dove was not the holy Ghost, nor yet the holy Ghost the dove: otherwise Angels, as we taught before, may enter secretly into a body which was made before, and which before had his being: as it is read of the Angel which spake in the asse of Balaam, and of the devil which spake unto Eve by the serpent. But of this kind we dispute not now; but only say, that Angels abiding after this manner in sensible creatures, are not joined to them in one and the self-same substance. Wherefore the asse could not be called an Angel, nor the Angel, an asse: no more than the serpent was in very deed the devil, or the devil a serpent. But the Son of God, for so much as he took upon him the nature of man, was man, and man was God, by reason of one and the self-same substance, wherein were two natures. Before which time, when he appeared unto Abraham, and unto the fathers, although he had true flesh; yet because the same was not joined in one substance with him, neither might he be called flesh,

neither was the flesh God. But afterward, when he took upon him both flesh and soul, so as there was only one substance or person, then might it be truly said that man was God, and God was man. By which means it came to pass, that he should verily be borne, that he should suffer death, and redeem mankind: wherefore he truly called himself The son of man. And in John he saith; Ye seek to kill me, a man that hath told you the truth. And in the scriptures it is said; Made of the seed of David. And Peter in the Acts; Ye have killed (saith he) a man ordained unto you of God. And Isaiah; Behold a virgin shall conceive, and shall bring forth a son.

These words have great force: for unless Christ had been very man, a virgin could not have conceived him, neither have brought him forth, nor yet have called him her son. This doth Tertullian considerately note; If he had been a stranger (saith he) a virgin could not either have conceived him, or borne him. Also the Angel saluted Marie on this manner; Fear not (saith he) for thou shalt conceive a son, &c. And Elizabeth said; How happeneth this to me, that the mother of my Lord cometh unto me? If she had had Christ only as a ghost, she might not be called his mother. Also the said woman said; Blessed be the fruit of thy womb. But how could it have been called the fruit of her womb, if he had brought a body with him from heaven? And in Isaiah it is written; A rod shall come forth of the stock of less, and a blossom shall flourish out of her root. Jesse was the stock, Marie was the root, and Christ was the blossom which took his body of hir. Matthew also thus beginneth his gospel; The book of the generation of Jesus Christ, the son of David, the son of Abraham. If Christ brought a body from heaven, how was he the son of Abraham, or of David? Moreover, the promise made to Abraham concerning Christ is on this wise; In thy seed shall all the nations of the earth be blessed. Paul entreating of these words in the epistle to the

Galatians; He said not (saith he) in seeds, as though in many; but in thy seed, which is Christ. And in the epistle to the Romans, we read; Of whom Christ came according to the flesh. All these sayings prove most evidently, that Christ was very man; and that in him was one substance of God and man. These things cannot be said of the Angels, nor yet of the son of God, before he was borne of the virgin: although when he appeared, he had very flesh, as we said before, but not joined to him in one and the self-same substance. Neither yet could it be said of the holy Ghost, that he was a very dove indeed; although the same, wherein he once appeared, was a very dove. And according to this sense wrote Tertullian those things that we cited before, which being not rightly understood, might breed either error or offense unto those that shall read them.

16. Now remaineth the other question; to wit, Whether Angels clothed with bodies taken, did eat and drink indeed? Of the Schoolmen some think that they did eat indeed, and some deny it. Scotus thinketh, that to eat, is nothing else but to chew meat, and to convey it down into the belly: but this did the Angels; wherefore he gathereth that they did verily eat. Others think, that to eat, is not only to chew the meat, or to convey it down into the belly; but further, to convert it into the substance of his own body, by concoction, through the quickening power: which thing, seeing the Angels did not, they did not truly eat. The book of Tobias is not in the canon of the Hebrews; but yet we might apply the same to our purpose, saving that there is a disagreement in the copies. For in that book which Munster set forth in Hebrew, in the twelfth chapter, the Angel Raphael said; I seemed to you to eat and to drink, but I did not eat, nor yet drink. The common translation hath; I seemed to you to eat and to drink, but I use invisible meat and drink. Neither text denieth, but that the Angel did eat after some manner. But whatsoever

may be gathered of these words, me thinketh that the interpretation of Augustine in his 13th book De trinitate, the 22nd chapter is to be received, where he wrote on this wise; The Angels did truly eat, yet not for need, but to procure conversation and familiarity with men. Wherefore when as in another text it is said, that Raphael did not eat, it must not so be understood, as though he did not eat at all, but that he did not eat after the manner of men. But this is specially to be noted there, that when the Angel answereth, that he doth feed upon invisible meat and drink; that spiritual food was nothing else, but a perfect and manifest knowledge of the true God, and an execution of his divine will. As Christ also said, that His meat was to do the will of his father. The very which also is our meat, although not after the same manner: for they see God manifestly, but we by a glass and in a dark speech.

17. We may call Angels (both according to the Greek and Hebrew name) messengers or legates, verily not as though they should teach God as concerning the affairs of men, or any other business: nay rather, to the intent that they themselves may be instructed, what they ought to minister, and show tidings of. If so be thou read in the scriptures, that they offer up our prayers, this is not done of them to instruct or teach God: in like manner, as we, when we pray fervently, do not therefore lay before God, our calamities, as though he were ignorant of them: seeing the Lord testifieth of that matter; that He knoweth whereof we have need, even before we ask. But by discovering and laying them open, we ourselves be the more earnestly bent to crave the help of God. And what discommodity should arise, if we affirm this self-same thing to come to pass in Angels? These things did Augustine write in his 15th book De trinitate, the 13th chapter. And in Enchiridio ad Laurentium, the 58th chapter, he saith the same thing, when he entreateth of the names of Angels, which are recited in the first chapter of the epistle to the

Colossians; Let them say what they can what be thrones, dominions, principalities, and powers; so they be able to prove that they say.

And against the Priscillianists, and Originists, the 11th chapter; Archangels (saith he) perhaps are powers, and we deny not, but that there is some difference between these; but to be ignorant of such a thing, will bring no great danger unto us. For there certainly are we in danger, where we despise the commandments of God, or neglect the obedience of him. But if thou wilt ask me, why the scriptures make mention of these things, if the knowing, or not knowing of them be of so small importance? He addeth a fit answer; namely, that If these things have been revealed to some excellent men, they may then know that there is nothing proved for a certainty, which is not found written in the scriptures. To which answer, I add also this other; Because we may be the more humble, and not to puff up ourselves, as though we were able to sound unto the depth of all that we read in the canonical scriptures.

18. The Jews have noted in the history of Jacob, that the scripture saith not that he went, and met with the Angels: but contrariwise, that the Angels met with him, and that they say was done for honor sake. And thereof they argue further, that Jacob, and every godly man is more worthy than Angels, forsomuch as the person that is met, is more honorable than he that goeth forth to meet. Also, he is better which is borne of any man, than he which beareth him. But the scripture saith, that the Angels do bear [the godly] in their hands, least they should hurt their feet against the stones. Who so ever is appointed to have the custody of another, seemeth to be inferior to him which is kept. By which reasons they make Angels inferior unto holy men, who are called The friends of God. But all men do easily see how these reasons of theirs do prove. For the father and the mother do bear in their arms their young children, do they therefore bear more worthy than themselves? It is said, that Christ

doth bear all things by the word of his power; but who is so far beside himself, or deceived, as to judge that things created, be more excellent than the Son of God? The shepherd when he findeth his sheep, beareth it upon his shoulders; doth he bear a better than himself? A father, a master, and a friend, go forth upon the way to meet with their son, scholar, or friend, returning from peril out of a strange country; do they this therefore as unto their better? Men be every-where set over flocks of sheep to keep them, yet are they much better than the sheep. In very deed the Angels do all these things, not that they are bound to us, but to the intent they may be thankful unto God. Wherefore the arguments of the Rabbins are vain and frivolous.

19. But unto this self-same purpose, there be reasons gathered out of the New Testament. For the Apostle saith in the first chapter to the Ephesians; Christ being raised up by his father from death, is lifted up on high, far above all principality, and power, and dominion, and above every name that is named, not only in this world, but also in the world to come. Further, in the second chapter he testifieth, that God hath taken us up together with him, and hath already made us to sit on the right hand with him: whereby it cometh, that we are accounted greater than the Angels. For if we sit hard by Christ, and he no doubt hath ascended above all creatures, the highest degree giveth also place unto us. Howbeit, this is yet a blunt argument, for it may be, that we shall sit with Christ in glory, taking the saying generally. It is sufficient that we be partakers of that glory. And it followeth not necessarily thereof, that we shall be superiors unto the Angels; unless that thou wilt understand, that the state of men shall then be so absolute and perfect, as they shall have no more need of the help of Angels. When they shall have God and Christ present, and salvation attained, to what purpose shall there be need of the ministry of holy spirits? Whereof understand this reason; If so be

that when Christ came, and poured out his spirit plentifully among the faithful, that same instruction of Angels was not used, or needful unto divine things, as commonly it had been in the Old Testament: even so in the everlasting kingdom, where we shall have Christ revealed, and the father evidently known unto us, certainly we shall enjoy the fellowship of Angels, but not use the ministry of them. But as touching the substance and nature of Angels, and of men, we cannot certainly know in what degree we and they shall be placed in the heavenly habitation: but yet, if we respect nature, we doubt not but that they are more excellent than we be. But who can boldly either affirm or deny, whether the grace and spirit of God shall more abound in some certain men than in them?

Nevertheless, as concerning the place of S. Paul in the second chapter to the Ephesians, it sufficeth, that his words be true; namely, that we, as we be, and are contained in our head, may be said to sit at the right hand of the father, above all creatures. But afterwards, if one would infer thereby [that we shall do the same] as touching our own proper nature or person, that cannot be proved by any firm argument. And Paul useth things past for things to come, to wit, that we are already taken up, and sit in heavenly places (and that not without reason) that he might make the same more certain, even as those things be which are past already. Or else, if we have respect to the will and decree of God, these things be already done. But in the epistle to Timothy, the self-same things are assigned unto the time to come, when the Apostle saith; If we be dead together with Christ, we shall live together with him: If we suffer with him, we shall also reign with him. Yet nevertheless, we must not accuse him of a lie, in that he useth those times that be past, instead of the times to come. For whatsoever is come to pass in our head, we confess it to be done in us; in so much verily, as we are grown up together with him. Wherefore let none say; If Christ be risen from death, if he be carried up into heaven, if he sit at the right hand of God, what belongeth this unto me? Yes doubtless, very much, for whatsoever hath happened unto him, thou mayest of good right esteem that it hath happened to thyself. Those shall not greatly trouble us, which by thrones, principalities, powers and dominions, will have to be understood such princes, monarchs, and magistrates. For Paul, when he maketh mention of these, speaketh manifestly of Angels, and of spirits that be above: whom in the second to the Ephesians, he calleth rulers or guiders of the world: and to the Colossians he saith; Christ hath spoiled principalities and powers, and hath led them as it were in open triumph. In which place who seeth not, that these words do signify unto us the spirits which be adversaries unto God?

20. But whereas it is said in the first to the Corinthians, the 15th chapter; When he hath put down all principality, and rule, and power: these things, as well Chrysostom, as diverse other interpreters, refer unto the devil, and other wicked spirits, being soldiers of his band; which I mislike not. Albeit, if any will understand them as concerning magistrates and principalities of this world, I will not be against it. For kings and princes have the sword, to the intent that sin may be kept in subjection; and that innocent subjects may be defended from violence and injuries: which things shall take no place, when things shall be set at peace and quietness by Christ. We might also under these names comprehend the good Angels, which be assigned as ministers and helpers unto us, while we be here in this miserable life; as we read in the epistle to the Hebrews, and as Daniel testifieth, they be set over kingdoms, and they be the guardians of men: seeing Christ said, as touching the young children; Their Angels do always behold the face of the Father. But when the kingdom of Christ shall be fully appeased, then these ministries shall be superfluous; and therefore it is said, that they shall be taken away. Yea, and the labors

of the sun, moon, stars, and celestial bodies shall not be needful: for therefore are they moved, and keep their circuit in the world, that they may drive away darkness and cold; and because that fruits also may be brought forth for the defense of our infirmity: which being perfectly healed, these helps and supportations shall be at rest. Wherefore we read in the Revelation of John, that an Angel sware by him that liveth forever, that hereafter there should be no time anymore: which cannot be taken away, unless the motions of the heavens be at rest. And therefore it is said, that all these things shall be abolished: if not as touching their substance, yet as touching their gifts and offices, which they exercise towards men. The same thing also may be said of ecclesiastical dignities and functions, which now indeed further unto edification: but when all things shall be perfect and absolute in the elect, they shall cease and have an end.

Many things hath Dionysius concerning the signification of the words Principality, power, and dominion; but yet such as are spoken only of him: for among the rest of the fathers, there is very little extant as touching these things; and that for good cause: for the holy scriptures teach not these things, because they further not to our salvation. Wherefore they, which be of the greatest judgment in ascribing of books to the true authors of them, do not think that Dionysius, which wrote of these things, is that Areopagita the scholar of Paul, but some later Dionysius. Neither is it likely to be true, that that work was in estimation long ago, seeing that (Gregory except, who was a Latin man) none of the ancient fathers cited those writings. I have heard sometimes diverse say, that these surnames of Angels were commonly translated by a metaphor taken of the powers of this world; and therefore they would that Paul, when he happened to make mention of Angels, remembered these names: as if he should say; Whether they be principalities or dominions. And they allege the place unto the Ephesians, where it is said; that Christ is set above every name that is named, whether it be in this life, or in the life to come. But I do not much allow this judgment, because not only the Rabbins, but also the holy scripture hath the name of Archangel, or Seraphim, and of Cherubim; which things declare, that among the celestial spirits there be certain orders and diverse offices.

21. Perhaps therefore the scripture, by the name of principality understands the higher spirits, unto whom is committed nothing but the charge of provinces, empires, and kingdoms. This meant Daniel, when he wrote of the prince of the Grecians, and of the Persians, and brought in Michaël the prince of God's people. Power, called in Greek <H&G>, is taken of Paul for that power, which is given of God to work miracles, whereby the wicked may be restrained: whereunto answereth on the other side, <H&G>, which signifieth The gift of healing. For even as by that power wicked men were chastened, so by this the vexed were made whole. By this power Peter slew Ananias and Zaphira, Paul made blind Elimas the sorcerer, and delivered diverse, which had sinned, into the hands of Satan. And those Angels in the eight chapter to the Romans, are called by this name, which be sent by God to punish the wicked. Such were they that destroyed Sodom and Gomorrah; and such was that Angel, which went between the host of the Egyptians, and the people of God, and which drowned Pharaoh with all his in the sea; and whom David saw upon the threshold of Areuna, destroying the people of God; and which consumed the host of Sennacherib with fire. Albeit God doth sometime the self-same things by evil Angels. For so David writeth in the psalm; that God sent plages among the Egyptians, by the hands of evil Angels. Paul [in that place to the Romans] nameth the orders of the Angels by their ministries and offices. And it is a thing worthy to be noted, that in the holy scriptures there be very few things mentioned of Angels: for subtly and earnestly to search after them, declareth rather

our curiosity, than furthereth our salvation. But those things which serve to edifying, are most diligently set forth in the scriptures: which thing I would to God that the Schoolmen had observed, for then they had not left behind them so many intricate and unprofitable things, which at this day are to no purpose, and with great offense disputed of. It is profitable for us to understand, that there be certain Angels appointed about our affairs; for by that means we perceive the goodness of God towards us. And on the other side also it is profitable to know, that there be some evil spirits, by whom we be continually assaulted; both, that we may beware of them, and that we may implore the help of God against them. And these things indeed, because they be profitable to be known, the holy scripture hath not kept them in silence.

Of the estate of man; In Gen. 2:7.

22. When thou hearest that God did shape man, think not only upon these outward parts or lineaments, but consider the inward parts; namely, the uppermost skin, the veins and sinews, the powers and passages, the bones, marrow, and these instruments of our life, which lie hidden within. But I consider three principal things in the creation of man. First, consultation; Let us make man. Secondly; God formed him of the dust. Thirdly; that He breathed in his face the breath of life. Thou shalt not read that it was so done in other living creatures. And yet thou mayest find the verb of making or forming in other places attributed unto the heavens, and to other things; namely, in the 95th psalm; His hands have formed the dry land. In the 45th of Isaiah; It is I that formed the light. In the seventh of Amos; He formed grasshoppers. But it is not the last or least dignity of man's body, that the same is of an upright stature. Whereof Ovid;

Where stooping unto earth, each beast doth downward bend:

A face upright to man he gave, to heaven for to tend.

And he formed him out of the earth. Wherefore the name of Adam, was of earth; as if thou shouldest say, sprung of the earth. Albeit some say, that it was of Adom, that is Red; because that earth was red. First therefore is formed the instrument, that is to wit, the body: next was added the mover, that is the soul, which should use the same. He breathed in his face or nostrils. For Appaiim first signifieth the nostrils; then, by the figure Synecdoche, by a part, the whole is taken for the countenance and face. Here it may signify both: first, the nostrils; because those, by drawing of breath, do chiefly show life: secondly, if thou understand it for the face, therein appear excellent tokens of the soul and of the life. Some would the metaphor to be taken from the forming of glasses. For by blowing thorough certain instruments they shape cups, boules, and diverse sorts of vessels. Howbeit, consider thou that here there is a metaphor, seeing God neither hath mouth, nor yet doth breath: even as he also hath no hands, by which he might frame men's bodies. But in these things it behooveth that thou understand the mighty power of God, his commandment, and most present strength. As touching the words Neschama, and Nephesch, they both of them sometime signify a blast of wind, or a breath: and otherwhile they be taken for substance, and for the soul, because the life is chiefly retained and showed by drawing of breath. Yea, and the Latin word Anima, that is the soul, is so called of wind and blast. In Greek it is <H&G>. It is also called of the Grecians <H&G>, of refrigeration or cooling. So as all these proper speeches may seem to have conspired together about the naming of the soul; that it should be so called of breathing out.

Hereupon, by reason of a double signification of the foresaid word, because it signifieth both the soul and a blast, there ariseth a double exposition. The first saith; By the commandment of God was the nostrils or face of man's body breathed into, and so he received life and soul: not that that blast was the soul, but a certain sign that the same should be planted in man by an outward beginning, and that the works of nature should not be expected, as the rest of the lives are had of other living creatures. And so we read in the Gospel, that Christ breathed upon the Apostles, and said; Receive ye the holy Ghost. And yet was not that blast the nature of the holy Ghost, but a sign thereof, that he would from without come into their souls, and that by the work of Christ. Again, in taking of that word for a blast, we might say, that God breathed; that is, he made man himself to breath; that is, after the body was made, he gave him the power of breathing: so as he being alive, and endued with a soul, might be seen and beheld. The second interpretation is, that that blast is taken for the soul, which is given unto us by God. And they say, that Nischmath. doth chiefly signify that which is divine and reasonable; that doth God give unto us. And where it is added; Man was made a living soul: Nephesch signifieth a sensible life, whereof other living creatures be partakers. Which thing plainly declareth unto us, that a soul reasonable is given unto us from above by God, and hath with it all power that other inferior creatures have.

Hence is excluded a double error. For we must not think, that the soul is of the substance of God, for that is invariable, and immutable: but the soul may become miserable, and it appeareth to be most inconstant. Furthermore, it is no blast of the nature and substance of the dying man: neither must it on the other side be accounted of the same quality and nature, that the lives be of other living creatures, because it is most certain, that in them is no understanding, seeing in the 32nd psalm, it is said of the horse and of the mule, that in them there is no understanding. And other beasts might think themselves wrongfully subdued unto men, if they had been endued with the same kind of soul. But this opinion needeth not to be confuted by many reasons, seeing the best philosophers were displeased therewith:

Look the propositions out of the second chapter of Genesis, in the end of this book.

23. But here they doubt, whether all the souls of men were created by God at the beginning, or else be made by him, and planted in bodies, according as the course of nature seemeth to require. There be some have thought, that they were all created at the beginning; among whom also there were many of the Jews. And among us Origin hath been reckoned of that opinion. And it seems that they were upon this cause moved hereunto; for that a reasonable soul being incorruptible, is not procreated of any matter. And therefore they say, that the same being by God made of nothing, it might not be truly said of him, that he rested the seventh day from all his work as touching creation. But this opinion hath no likelihood of truth. For seeing the soul is the lively part and form of the body, it seemeth that the bringing forth of them should be both joined together. Moreover, I would demand whether they be idle, or do something, all the while that they have their being before the body? If thou say that they be idle, it seemeth absurd, that things should be so long time destitute of their working. But if so be they do something, that must of necessity be either good or evil. But the scripture in the ninth to the Romans, pronounceth plainly of Jacob and Esau, that before they had done either good or evil.

But that which moveth more, is the history of the creation, which showeth unto us, that the soul was made even when the body was wrought out of the earth. For seeing there is no mention made thereof before, and that the production of so notable a thing should not have been kept in silence, it remaineth to be understood, that it was made by God even then, when we read, that it was inspired or blown in by him. But that reason, which concerneth the ceasing from all his labor, we may easily answer, if we say, that now also God doth work, either through the continual government of things; or else because, whatsoever things he maketh, are referred to the former, and be of the same kind that those be which were made in the first six days. But why the body was first made before the soul, this reason is showed by the fathers: because, if the soul should have been brought in before the body, it might have been idle, being without the organ and instrument of his actions. But this order hath God observed, that always should be first prepared those things, wherein the more excellent things should abide; and then to bring in the things themselves, that they might work so soon as ever they be made. First the earth was discovered from the waters, then the Sun and the Moon were made, which should exercise their power and strength upon the earth and plants thereof. All beasts were first made, and all the springs and plants of the earth; and last of all, man, which should be set over all these things, that immediately after he was created, he might have somewhat to do. In like manner now, the body is first, and then followeth the soul, least it should be idle. By which purpose of God we are taught, that among us this also may be done, that the more any men do excel, the more ready matter of working is ministered unto them, least they should live idly.

24. Moreover, man (saith Ibn-ezra) being made a living soul, he straightway moved himself: the first man was not created to be weak as young children be, which cannot guide themselves and walk; but after the manner of other living creatures, which walk immediately after they be brought forth:) or else he showed the tokens of the presence of the soul; moving (I mean) and sense. For these two (as Aristotle affirmeth) seemed to all the ancient philosophers to be the chief effects of the soul. Of this blast of God upon the dust or clay, whereof the body of man

was compact (we perceiving the same to be so mighty, as it quickened forthwith, and gave strength to all members) there is gathered a good argument for the easiness of our resurrection. For if his spirit shall blow again upon the ashes of the dead, they shall most easily put on again their souls, as it is described in the 37th chapter of Ezekiel, where he showeth, that by the breath of the spirit of God those bones were quickened; which last renewing of bodies, shall so far excel this, as Paul calleth this first man Of the earth, earthy; and the latter he calleth both spiritual and heavenly.

25. But let us see how it is true that is avouched [in the ninth of Genesis] that the blood is the soul. This the Manichees cannot abide in the Old Testament, and reprove it as a lie: for they utterly renounce the old books. And that which is written in Genesis, Leviticus, and Deuteron. they taunt with these arguments. In the first to the Corinthians the 15th chapter it is said; Flesh and blood shall not inherit the kingdom of God, therefore blood is not the soul: otherwise Paul had excluded souls out of the kingdom of heaven. Further, Christ in the gospel saith; Fear not those which kill the body, and have not to do with the soul: if so be that the blood be the soul, then without controversy, the tyrants have to do with it, they shed it, they destroy it, &c: while they kill the holy martyrs of God. These arguments are two manner of ways dissolved by Augustine against Adimantus. In the Old Testament the speaking is of the lives of brute beasts, but the arguments, which these men bring out of the New Testament, conclude as touching a reasonable and human soul: wherefore their own argument hath reproved them unawares. But the more thoroughly to confute their first argument, note, that when Paul in that place speaketh of the resurrection to come, he by flesh and blood meaneth, that the conditions of a mortal body shall be taken away from the saints at the resurrection. Which thing, the words alleged there

by him do declare; It is sown in corruption and mortality, but it shall rise again in contrary conditions.

But thou imaginest, that as well the life of brute beasts, as the souls of men are called blood. That must be a figurative speech, to be interpreted by the figure Metonymia, as it were the sign put for the thing signified. In like manner as Augustine testifieth against Adimantus; the Lord doubted not to say, This is my body, when he gave the sign of his body. Seeing therefore the blood is a sign of the presence of the soul, therefore it may be called the soul itself. Again, as by the same figure, the thing containing is taken for the thing contained. For who is ignorant, that the soul of man is after a sort contained in the blood, which being spilled and consumed, it cannot abide any longer in the body: yea, and it is so joined to the same, as it followeth in a manner the affections, and perturbations thereof so long as we live in this life. Yea, and some have thought that it was therefore decreed, that men should refrain from eating of blood, least they should become of beastly manners; which they say are easily carried into our mind, if we should eat the blood of wild beasts: which thing I have alleged, not as though I allow this to be the cause why God gave that commandment, but to declare the conjunction even of man's soul with the body.

26. But how man is the image of God, it is declared at the beginning of Genesis, where it is written, that God said; Let us make man after our image and likeness, that he may have dominion over the fowls of the air, the fishes of the sea, and the beasts of the earth. Where it appeareth, that herein standeth the image of God, that he should be ruler over all creatures, even as God is the ruler over all things. Augustine doth oftentimes refer this to the memory, mind and will, which being faculties of one and the self-same soul, do represent (as he saith) the three persons in one substance. Howbeit this doctrine of Augustine, doth rather show

the cause of the image. For man is not set above other creatures, to have dominion over them, for any other cause, but in respect that he is endued with reason, which plainly showeth itself by these three faculties. But yet this is not all that the image of God is bound unto. For it is not enough to govern and rule well the creatures of God, with memory, mind, and will; except we both understand, remember, and will those things, which be pleasing unto God. For if our mind remain infected, as it is, with sin; it will not lawfully have dominion of things, but will rather exercise tyranny against them. Wherefore the image of God is the new man, which understandeth the truth of God, and is desirous of the righteousness thereof; as Paul hath taught us, when he writeth to the Colossians; Put upon you the new man, which is shaped again in the knowledge of God, according to the image of him which created him. Where we see, that the knowledge of God is true and effectual, to lead unto the image of perfection. And this is more expressly set forth in the epistle to the Ephesians; Put you on the new man, which is created according to God, in righteousness and true holiness. When our mind is both endued with the knowledge of God, and adorned with righteousness, then doth it truly express God. For righteousness, and the knowledge of divine things are nothing else, but a certain flowing in of the divine nature into our minds.

But perhaps thou wilt urge, that after this manner a woman also is the image of God. We say, that if thou compare her with the rest of the creatures, she is the image of God; for she hath dominion over them, and hath the use of them. But in this place thou must compare her unto man, and then is she not said to be the image of God, because she doth not bear rule over the man, but rather obeyeth him. Wherefore Augustine in the 13th chapter of his book De trinitate said; If it be understood of man and woman, in respect that they be endued with mind and reason, it is meet that they should be according unto the image of God: but the woman being compared unto man, as touching the actions and affairs of this life, she is not the image of God, because she was created to be a helper of man. And in the same place he hath another exposition, but the same allegorical. He saith, that we be called men, seeing we contemplate God; and that we are of good right bare headed, because we must there repose ourselves with incessant endeavor: for unsearchable is the end of divine things. But we are called women (saith he) when we descend with our cogitations unto the care of earthly things. There it is meet to have the head covered, because a measure must be used, and we must take heed, that we be not too much plunged in worldly things. Howbeit we must not lean unto allegorical interpretations. The exposition which we alleged before is plain.

Of the image of God, look more in the propositions out of the first and second chapters of Gen. in the end of this book.

27. The image of any man is the form, whereby it representeth him. A similitude of any man is a quality, wherein it resembleth him. What this image then is, let us most absolutely declare. A man not only hath the power and strength of understanding, whereby he is not far from God; but he is also created with most excellent and heavenly qualities. He is endued with justice, wisdom, mercy, temperance, and charity. But the very full image of God, is Christ, as touching his divine nature; and further, as concerning his human nature, so much as there can be of the similitude of God in it: as appeareth in the first to the Hebrews, the first to the Colossians, and in the eight chapter to the Romans. Again; This is my well-beloved son in whom I am well pleased. We were made, to the end we should be such: for we have understanding, and are capable of divine perfections. In them we were made, but we cannot be restored unto them, unless it be by the help and example of Christ, who

is the principal and true image. How much we be the image of God, it appeareth by our felicity, which we have one and the same with our God; I mean, in loving and knowing. But if thou demand, by what power men rule over things? Doubtless not by bodily strength: for as touching that, the most part of living creatures exceed us. Wherefore this is done by reason, counsel, and art: by which man not only mastereth and taketh these living creatures, but he also moveth and changeth exceeding great and weighty things. This power is chiefly restored by faith; Thou shalt walk upon the adder and dragon: Psal. 91. Daniel was cast unto the lions; Christ lived among wild beasts in the wilderness; Paul took no harm by the viper; Samson and David overcame the lions.

As touching this dominion over beasts, there ariseth a difficulty; wherefore were these wild beasts made, that they should be a trouble unto men? I answer, to the intent that wicked children might be chastened. After sin, a scourge was meet for him; sin armed our own servants against us: for which cause the irruption and invasion of beasts was sent, as testifieth the scripture in the fifth of Ezekiel; I will send hunger and wicked beasts among you. Unto the righteous man all appeared to be meek and quiet. And now, albeit that they have rebelled, yet it happeneth that very few perish thereby. And if any man be destroyed by them, there cometh profit unto us two manner of ways by it. First, it is an example of the severity of God, as in the Samaritans, which were slain by the lions; the second book of Kings, the 17th chapter: in the children which were killed by the bears, because they mocked Elisha; the second book of Kings, the second chapter: in the disobedient prophet, which the lion killed: the first of Kings, the 13th chapter. Furthermore, it is showed how great the majesty of God is, that even the wild beasts do revenge the injury done unto him. Lastly, behold here with me the goodness of God towards us, which hath bounded this hurtful cattle within the precincts

of the desert and solitary places, and in a manner permitted them to
wander but only in the night. Here also may man see his calamity after
sin, that he being such and so notable a creature, should perish with the
sting of one little silly scorpion, or by the biting of a mad dog. But yet
nevertheless, the wild beasts have not been able, in respect of sin, utterly
to shake off the yoke of men; they fear and tremble at the sight of him,
yea, and thou mayest see a child to rule, beat, and threaten the greatest
beasts. In him they do reverence the image of God.

28. This image is not properly meant as touching the body, seeing God
is not of bodily substance; yet is it not far from the similitude of God,
seeing as an instrument it expresseth many similitudes of God, which
lie hidden in the soul. But there were some among the Hebrews, which
affirmed that this was also spoken as concerning the body, if thou shalt
respect those images and similitudes, wherein God showed himself to
be seen unto the Patriarchs and Prophets. For he appeared as the son
of man, the first chapter of Ezekiel, the seventh chapter of Daniel, and
the sixth of Isaiah. Which reason of theirs, if it were to be allowed, we
say that this was the rather true, by reason of the incarnation of Christ;
to wit, that such a body was given unto man, as God did beforehand
determine, that his word should take upon him. But (as I have said)
this is understood of the inward man; namely, of the soul, whereof the
body is the instrument, and therefore not altogether strange from that
similitude. Wherefore thou hast here the true knowledge of man. Man
is a creature of God, formed according to the image of his maker. By
which declaration, not only his nature endued with reason is known, but
also his properties, and his end; namely felicity, that according to this his
constitution, he should live in such actions, as may express the image of
God.

Hereupon depend the laws, both of nature and of man, even that this image may be restored and preserved, that man may keep free dominion. Hereof it cometh, that of this excellent state, and condition of man's nature, proceedeth all virtues; as to be just, valiant, and endued with charity. From this condition of man's nature we may gather, that virtues are engrafted in man by nature: and that the arguments, whereby Aristotle in his second book of Ethics proveth the contrary, taketh place in this our corrupted nature. Thou mayest also consider the goodness of God, for that the felicity of man (over and besides the excellent actions of virtue) requireth abundance of outward things, seeing those be instruments; for by riches, as by instruments, we do many things: and therefore God would at the beginning adorn the first man, with such great riches and empire. Also man by this place is admonished of his duty, manner and form of all his actions. How often soever he is about to do anything, let him say with himself: Is this to show my father? Is this to live according to the image? By this also we learn, how convenient is our deliverance by Christ. For seeing our perfection consisteth in this, that we should retain the image of God, which was obscured by the fault of our first parents, it was very meet, that the same should be again imprinted in men by Christ, that is, by his spirit, which is the very lively image of God. And hereby we may learn, what dignity the Church of God is of; what manner of citizens it hath, and requireth; namely, such as be like unto God: finally, when thou hearest that God created man, thou must call to mind as touching the body, the whole workmanship of all the instrumental parts, and the commodities and ornaments of the several members: and as touching the soul, all the powers, qualities, and actions which are found therein.

Of Paradise.

29. It is said, that God planted Paradise in Heden. But this word Paradise, although it be common as well to the Greeks as to the Hebrews,

yet in very deed it is a Hebrew word, since Solomon used the same in Ecclesiastes the second chapter: and it signifieth a garden. So great a care had God of man, whom he had created, as he would have him set in a place of the greatest pleasure and delight. Heden in the second chapter of Genesis signifieth a region, so called by reason of the pleasant and delectable soil. And that the same was a region, we gather by diverse places. In the fourth chapter of Genesis it is said of Cain, that he lived like a runagate in the land of Nod eastward from Heden. And in the 27th chapter of Ezekiel there is mention made of the children of Heden, which are joined with Chamne and Charam. And we know that Charam is a region of Mesopotamia, unto which Abraham went, when he came forth of his country. So likewise we read of the children of Heden, in the 37th chapter of Isaiah: wherefore it is not only known to be a region; but by the reading of these prophets, we conjecture the coast and site wherein it is. Further, of the garden of Heden, there is oftentimes mention made in the holy scriptures; but that is by a manner of comparison, when the pleasantness of any place is to be expressed, as in the second of Joel, in the 51st of Isaiah, and in the 28th of Ezekiel. Wherefore (in mine opinion) they are very much deceived, which will understand all things here by allegory: for it was a garden indeed, planted by the commandment of God.

Neither are they to be heard, which seek for such a paradise upon the highest mountains, so as they would have the same to be near the moon, or under the equinoctial line, by reason of the temperature of the air. Which opinion is disproved by these things, which we have said. It was planted by God in a certain region, which is not far from Mesopotamia. The history also is declared by Moses; wherefore we must not make a mere allegory thereof. It is said, that it was planted in the oriental part: which nevertheless some understand; From the beginning: seeing under that word, both may well be signified. The Hebrew interpreters (for the most part) understand it of the east situation, whom the seventy interpreters by their exposition do allow. Albeit they think (and it seemeth not absurd) that this garden was planted by the power of God the third day, when the rest of the green trees, plants, and herbs were brought forth; but yet placed in the second chapter, when the history of man's creation is set forth. Indeed that garden was appointed for the habitation of man. Howbeit this is but a small controversy; whether the same were planted the third day, or on the sixth, it maketh no great matter.

Look the propositions out of the fourth chapter of Gen. at the end of this book.

30. Out of the region, wherein paradise was set, there issued forth a river or fountain, which went into the garden, and watered the same: and from thence it was divided into four branches. Whereabout this division is made, whether at the departing out of paradise, or at the very breaking forth from Heden, it doth but little appear by the words: but the greater part do judge, that it is to be thought, that it issueth forth from the entrance of paradise. Two of the names of the rivers be certain, and two be doubtful. As touching Euphrates and Tigris, which compass about Mesopotamia, there is no doubt. As concerning Physon and Ghihon what they are, the interpreters do vary. But by our writers Physon is taken for Ganges; but it is Nile, whose original is so uncertain, as thereof hath risen a proverb (touching them which inquire after things that be very doubtful) that They seek the head of Nile. If there be any things reported of the beginning thereof, they are very uncertain; and (as many do affirm) it may arise in some other place, than it seemeth to do, and afterward break out through hollow places and parts under the earth, unto that place which seemeth now to be the fountain and head thereof: that no doubt is Nile. The fourth river Ghihon is thought of many to

be Nile; which thing I think not to be true. For in the first of Kings, the first chapter, David commandeth that his son Solomon should be conveyed to Ghihon, which river the Chaldean interpreter translateth Syloa, whereof there is mention in the Gospel, and in Isaiah. And it is said, that it watereth the whole land of Ethiopia; not that Ethiopia which is in Egypt, but perhaps the Midianites and Ethiopians, which were neighbors to the Israelites; from whence was Ziphora an Aethiop woman, the wife of Moses, who nevertheless is said to be a Madianite. Wherefore by these known names of the rivers it is manifest, that paradise was in a certain region of the east part.

And we must not forget, that the word paradise is translated, to signify the state of eternal felicity: as when Christ said to the thief; This day shalt thou be with me in paradise. And Paul in the first to the Corinthians, the 12th chapter saith, that he was raptured up into paradise. The metaphor is plain, and very comfortable; as who would say, that is a pleasant and delectable garden, where it shall be lawful for us to enjoy God. Whereupon the Gentiles account their fields Elysii as gardens, [where they imagined the souls of good men to dwell.] But let us return to our terrestrial Heden. What is become thereof at this day? There be some which think, that it is yet extant, and that the place cannot be come unto. Others think, that it is no more to be found; unto which opinion I might easily subscribe. For seeing that place was assigned unto man, when he was innocent; he ceasing to be such a one, unto what use should the garden serve? Wherefore this place either was taken away, when the flood drowned the world; or else immediately after the curse given to the man, the woman, and the serpent, when as the earth also was cursed, and then all those pleasures and delights perished. Against which opinion that nevertheless may seem to be, which is spoken of the Cherubim, that was set with a two-edged sword for keeping of the same. But it may be answered, that this was then done for the terrifying of Adam; or else that kind of custody remained until Noah's flood. These things may we declare unto you, out of the saying of diverse interpreters; when as yet there is no certain determination made of this thing out of the holy scriptures.

That Adam used the Hebrew speech it is noted upon Gen. the first, verse the eight. And of the confusion of tongues, look the eleventh chapter of Genesis. Also if any be desirous to know the original of diverse nations and countries, let him read in Genesis, the tenth chapter, and Judge. 12:6.

Of the long life of the Fathers.

31. But some men might muse in their mind, how it happened that the old Fathers before the flood, and a while after lived so long; and that this age afterward was shortened by little and little, until it was brought by a common course unto fourscore years? Many were the causes of that long life in the old time. [And it hath been the general opinion, as well among the philosophers as Divines, that those ancients lived all that while by nature, and not miraculously. [1] And the first reason that moved them thereunto, was; that our first parents Adam and Eve were created immediately by the hand of God, without any means of man, or of any other corruptible thing: wherefore it is presupposed, that he made them of an excellent complexion, of a perfect agreement, and proportion of humors: by which means the children proceeding from them, resembled their parents in sound and good complexion, until the third generation. [2] Secondly, in those days they had no such cause to breed diseases and infirmities, as did afterward follow to their succession. [3] Thirdly, their temperance in eating and drinking, as well in quantity as in quality, did much further them; because they were not acquainted with the eating of flesh, nor yet with the confection of so many dainty

dishes, as we are in these days. [4] Furthermore, in those days, fruits, plants and herbs were of more virtue than now they be, because they sprang from a new made ground, and as yet became not barren with the inundation of waters. [5] Also Adam out of all doubt knew the property of all herbs and plants, for the preservation of health, more than we at this day do, and brought the same knowledge to his succession after him. [6] Moreover, the course of the heavens, and the influence of the stars and planets were then more favorable unto them, than they be now unto us, when as they have passed so many eclipses, aspects and conjunctions; whereof proceedeth so great alterations and changes upon the earth.] [7] Besides this, many children were then to be procreated, and the world to be replenished, which was done by the means of long life. [8] Arts were to be found out, wherefore long life was requisite; for they are learned by experience. [9] And (that which was the chiefest cause) it behooved that the worshipping of the only true God should be retained among men; which thing in so great a variety of people might hardly have been done. Afterward, when so great a procreation was not needful, when arts were found out, and the holy scriptures (unto which the service of God was fastened) were given unto us, long life would have been tedious. The patriarch Jacob said; Few and evil are the days of thy servant, if they should be compared unto the age of our forefathers, not to our age. So this shortening of man's age, was done of a certain mercy of God towards us.

But why did those first men abstain so long from procreation of children? For it is written, that they begat children at the age of five hundred years, at a hundred and thirty, and not before. Augustine in the 15th book De civitate Del, the 15th chapter saith, that It may be answered two manner of ways; the first is, that in these men it was long before they came to the age of procreation, and that they enjoyed not the power of seed so soon as we do. Which answer may thus be confirmed; our age is divided into infancy, childhood, youth, and man's state. Wherein if so be the number of years be proportioned to the rate of our whole age, so was it then. And therefore, if their life did so greatly exceed ours, it behooved also that the time of their infancy and childhood should be more at length extended and enlarged. The second answer is, that in that genealogy, the descent is not reckoned from one first begotten to another. For it may be, that there were others begotten even before them; which thing is after this manner declared. The purpose of the scripture is to convey the course of the narration unto Abraham, from whom the people of Israel had their beginning: wherefore in the genealogy those children are chosen to be described, by whom they descend unto him. But it is of no necessity, that those had been of the first begotten. Even as in the gospel of Matthew, where the meaning of the Evangelist, in describing of the stock of Christ, is to descend by David unto Christ himself, therefore he doth not always take the first begotten; for Ishmael was borne before Isaac, Esau went before Jacob: and in the order of the procreation, Judah among the children of Jacob was not the first begotten. And by Judah himself other children were begotten, before Phares and Zeram of Tamar. Neither was David the eldest son of his father, but the youngest among the rest of his brethren. But by others, the stock would not have descended unto Christ. But why specially it was so long before that Noah begat children, was (as saith Rabbi Selomoh) because that the children, which should have been begotten before of him, might easily have been infected with the vices of other men. And God would that they, at the time of the flood, should be younger, whereby they might not be infected with such horrible vices as others were.

Finally, it is thus argued; These, if they had been borne long before the flood, would either have been just or wicked; if they had been wicked, they must therefore have perished with others, and by that means sorrow had been added unto a righteous father, which thing God would not; if they had been good, and they also had begotten others, and perhaps Noah himself others also: all which, if God would have saved for Noah's sake, the ark should have been made much bigger. Whereby Noah had been more wearied, in the building of it, than reason would. This seemeth to be a pleasant devise. But (as I have said before) it shall appear sufficiently to a Christian man, that either these were not the first among his children, or else that children were denied him, so long as it pleased the Lord. Neither is it meet to cleave unto fables, so curiously invented. But what shall we say as concerning the great number of years, wherein they are said to have lived? Shall we be so hardy to affirm, that those were not so long as these years of ours, but that they were of two or three months long? And Pliny seemeth to report in the 7th book of his natural history, that diverse countries made their computation of years otherwise than we do; and that thereby it came to pass, that some may seem to have lived longer than the common course. This cannot possibly be proved by this argument; because in the description of the ark, and of the flood, there is mention made of the second and tenth month: wherefore the same manner of years was then that are now. [Yea and by the whole course of the history ye may plainly perceive, that the full number of days and months, which we use in our age (or at the least wise within very few more or less) were completed at that time. For in the 17th day of the second month, at what time as the fountains of the great deep did break up, Noah entered into the ark. The 17th day of the second month, the ark rested upon the tops of Armenia. In the first day of the tenth month, the tops of the mountains were seen; then followed forty days before Noah opened the window of the ark; whereunto add 14 days more, which were spent in sending forth of the dove. Which

being in all 54 days, or two months, make up the full number of twelve
months; the very same reckoning which we at this day observe. So we
have it sufficiently proved, that seeing as well the years as months of old
time were the very same that ours be, or little differing, the time of their
life in those days was no less, than the scriptures declare.]

Look the propositions out of the fourth chapter of Gen. at the end of
this book.

Of Giants.

32. Now, seeing that in the holy scriptures, there is mention made
oftentimes of giants, it shall not be unprofitable if we speak somewhat
of them. First we must understand, that they be called by diverse names
in the scriptures, as Rephaim, Nephilim, Emim, and Hanakim. The
Hebrew verb Hanak, is to environ or compass about, and from thence
is derived the noun Hanak: and in the plural number it is both the
masculine and feminine gender, and signifieth a chain; and it is transferred unto notable and famous men: as if thou shouldest say Knight and
chainmen. But they were called Emim, by reason of a terror which they
brought upon others with their look. They were called Zamzumim, of
wickedness; for they having confidence in their own power and strength,
contemned both laws, justice, and honesty; and they always wrought
wickedness. For doubtless the Hebrew word Zimma, signifieth wickedness, or mischief. Also they were named Rephaim, because men meeting
with them, became in a manner astonished: for that word otherwhile
signifieth dead men. Finally they be called Nephilim, as one may say
oppressors, of the verb Naphal, which is To fall or to rush upon; because
they did violently run upon all men. Som thought that they were sometime called Gibborim; but because we use to refer that word unto power,
and Gibborim are properly called strong men; therefore I would not put
it among these. Further, if thou wilt demand when giants began to be (to

follow the opinion of Augustine in the 16th book De civitate Dei, the 23rd chapter) we may say that they were before the flood. Wherein we believe him, because he proveth it by the testimony of the holy scriptures: for we have it in the sixth of Genesis, that in those days there were giants upon the earth, whose stock although it were preserved after the flood, yet he thinketh that it was not in any great number.

33. Besides this, there is a doubt as touching procreation and parents. For some think that they were not begotten of men, but that angels or spirits were their parents: and this they say, is specially confirmed by that which is written in the book of Genesis; The sons of God seeing the daughters of men, that they were fair, took them to wives, and of them were borne most mighty men or giants. Of this fall of angels, because they were conversant with women, many of the ancient fathers are of one mind: and among the rest Lactantius in the second book the 15th chapter. For (as we read there) he thought, that God feared least that Satan, to whom he had granted dominion of the world, would utterly have destroyed mankind: and therefore he gave unto mankind angels for tutors, by whose industry and care they might be defended. But they being as well provoked by the craft of Satan, as allured by the beauty of fair women, committed uncleanness with them; wherefore he saith, that both they were cast from their dignity, and were made soldiers of the devil. This indeed did Lactantius think; yet he said not, that through those meetings of the angels with women, were born giants; but earthly Daemons or spirits, which walk about the earth to our great harm. Eusebius Caesariensis, in his fifth book De praeparatione evangelica, is in a manner of the same opinion. For he saith also, that the angels which fell, begat of women (whom they lewdly loved) those Daemons or spirits, which afterward in sundry wise brought great troubles to the world. And to the very same sort he referreth all those, which the poets

and historiographers taught to be gods: and whose battles, contentions, lusts, sundry and great tumults, they have mentioned either in verse or in prose.

But Augustine De civitate Dei, the 15th book, and 23rd chapter, thinketh not that the opinion of these ancient fathers can be gathered out of that place of Genesis. For he saith, that such as be there called The sons of God, were very men, and came of the generation of Seth, the third son of Adam. For seeing they retained the true and sincere religion of God, and the pure invocation of his name, and were adorned with the favor and grace of God; they are called by the scriptures The children of God. Nevertheless, when they afterward burned in the lusting after those women, which descended of the stock of Cain, and therefore belonged to the society of the wicked, and had taken to themselves wives of them, they themselves also inclined to superstitions and ungodly worshipping's; and they of the sons of God not only became men, but also flesh. And (to show this by the way) Aquila translating those words out of the Hebrew; Not (saith he) the sons of God, but the sons of gods, in this respect (as I think) because they had godly progenitors, which so miserably fell from God, through the mad love of women. But Symmachus translateth it; The sons of the mighty. But to return to Augustine, he constantly affirmeth, that out of that place of Genesis, there can be nothing gathered, as touching the copulation of angels with women: but rather thinketh, that far otherwise may be gathered of the words of God there written. For when the scripture had there said, that giants were upon the earth, and that the sons of God (as it is said) had transgressed and brought forth giants, it is added; And God said, My spirit shall not always strive with man, because he is flesh. By this saying Augustine will have it manifest, that they which so offended, are called men; not only as they were in their own nature, but also as they are called flesh, unto the which they inclined with their shameful lusts.

But they which understand it otherwise, think that they bring a great testimony of Enoch the seventh from Adam, of whom Jude speaketh in his canonical epistle. For in the book which is entitled to him, the giants are said to have had, not men, but angels to be the authors of their generation. But unto this answereth Augustine, that the book is altogether Apocryphus, [not canonical;] and therefore that credit must not be given to the fables, which be recited therein. He saith, that it must not be doubted, but that Enoch wrote many divine things, seeing Jude the apostle did plainly testify the same; but yet that it is not necessary to believe all the writings in the book of Apocryphus, which are showed to have come from him; forsomuch as they lack sufficient authority. Neither should it be thought, that if Jude uttered some certain sentence out of it, that therefore by his testimony he approved the whole book: unless thou wilt say, that Paul also allowed of all things that were written by Epimenides, Aratus, and Menander; because he alleged one or two verses out of them. Which thing Jerome in expounding of the first chapter of the epistle to Titus, testifieth to be a very absurd and ridiculous thing. And as concerning Enoch, it would seem a very great marvel, if he were the seventh from Adam, how he could write that Michael wrestled with the devil for the body of Moses; seeing if these things were (as in very deed we must believe they were) they of necessity happened well-near a thousand, five hundred years after; unless we shall grant that this was revealed unto him at that time, by a certain excellent power of prophesy.

34. Neither must it be forgotten, that those, which think that giants had not men, but angels for their parents, were therefore brought thus to think; because they thought it might not possibly be, that huge giants can be borne of men, which be of an ordinary stature and bigness. Wherefore

there were some, which proceeded so far in the matter, as they affirmed, that the first man was a giant; and also Noah and his children. For they believed not, that that kind of men, either before or after the flood (if so be they might be thought to have sprung of men) could be, unless they had such progenitors. But Augustine proveth that opinion to be false, and saith; that A little before the destruction which the Goths made, there was in Rome a woman of a giants stature, whom to behold, they came by heaps out of diverse parts of the world; which woman neverthe-less had parents, that exceeded not the common and usual stature of men. If we shall search what the cause is, that nature hath brought forth giants of such huge bodies; we can allege no other, but an abundance of natural heat, and a moisture, which abundantly and largely ministereth matter. For the heat, not only extendeth a man to tallness and height, but also spreadeth and enlargeth him to breadth and thickness. Wherefore giants began to be before the flood, and they were also before the resort which the sons of God had with the daughters of men, and were bred after that also. Further, men did beget them, and there was a natural cause, as I have showed. Also for a truth, there were of them borne after the flood. For there is mention made of them in the books of Numbers, Deuteronomy, Joshua, Judges, Samuel, and Paralipomenon, and in others of the holy books.

35. Of the greatness and stature of them, we may partly conjecture, and partly we have the same expressly described. The conjectures be, that Goliath had a coat of male, which weighed fifty thousand sickles of brass. The haft of his spear was like a weavers beam, and the iron spear had weighed six hundred sickles of iron. We also conjecture of the exceeding great stature of Og the king of Basan, by his bed, which being of iron, was of ten cubits long. Also, the Israelites being compared with Anachis, seemed to be but grasshoppers: these things may be a token

unto us, of what greatness these men were. But the greatness of Goliath is properly and distinctly set forth in the book of Samuel: for it is said there, that he was of six cubits and a hand-breadth high: and a cubit, if we follow the measure of the Greeks, is two foot; but according to the account of the Latins, one foot and a half. Some allege this to be the cause of the difference; that the measure may be sometimes extended from the elbow to the hand, sometime closed together, and sometime open and stretched forth. This is as much as I could gather of the stature of giants out of the holy scripture. But among the Ethnics we read of much more wonderful things, such as men can hardly be persuaded to give credit unto. For Pliny writeth in his seventh book, that in Candie there fell down a hill, and that there was found a man's body of six and forty cubits long, which some thought to be the body of Orion, some of Otho. Also it is written, that the body of Orestis, being digged up, by the commandment of an oracle, was of 7 cubits. That which Berosus affirmeth of Adam, and of Seth his son, and of Noah and his sons, that they were all giants, seeing it is without scripture, it may be rejected. Philostratus saith in his Heroikes, that he saw a certain dead carcass of a giant of thirty cubits long, another of two and twenty, and another of twelve. But the common stature of men in these days is little above five foot. And herein the measure of a foot agreeth as well among the Greeks as Latins, that unto every foot are appointed four hand-breadths, and every hand-breadth containeth the breadth of four fingers, that is, the length of the little finger. But if so be that the two outward most fingers, I mean the thumb and the little finger be stretched out, every foot containeth only two spans or hand-breadths. Unto this place I thought good to transfer those things, which Augustine hath in his 15th book De civitate Dei, the ninth chapter, where he reproveth those, which affirm stoutly, that men were never of such tall stature; and showeth, that he himself saw upon the coast of Utica, a cheek-tooth of a man so exceeding great, as the same being divided into the form and quantity of usual teeth in our age, it might easily be judged a hundred times greater. And that there were many such personages in old time, he declareth out of the verses of Virgil in the 12th book of Aeneidos, where he brought in Turnus to have lifted up from the earth, and to have shaken at Aeneas so great a stone, as twelve choice men could scarcely rule.

He said no more, but straight a mighty stone be there beheld,
A mighty ancient stone, that then by chance within the field
There for a bownd did lie, all strife twixt lands for to appease,
Scarce could twelve chosen men that on their shoulders lift with ease.
Such men (I mean) as nowadays the earth to light do bring,
This up in hand he caught, and tumbling at his foe did fling.

Which thing he declared out of the sixth Iliad of Homer. Also Virgil in the first book of Georgicks saith, that men would wonder in time to come, when they should happen to till up the fields of Aematia, to see the greatness of bones which should be digged out of the graves. Further, he alledgeth Pliny the second, who in the seventh book affirmeth, that nature, the further forward that it goeth, the lesser bodies it daily bringeth forth. He calleth to mind, that Homer once in his verses bewailed the self-same thing, whereunto I might add the testimony of Cyprian against Demetrianus. But if I should be demanded, whether I think that men's bodies, which came after the flood, were less than those which were brought forth before the flood perhaps I would grant they were: but that they have continually decreased, even from the flood to this day, that I would not easily grant; especially considering the words which Aulus Gellius wrote in his third book, where he saith; that The stature whereunto man's body groweth, is of seven foot, which seemeth also at this day to be the measure of the taller statures. But yet we read in the

Apocryphus of Esdras in the fourth book, at the end of the fifth chapter, that now also our bodies are less, and daily shall be lessened; because nature always becometh more barren. The self-same thing also (as I said a little before) Cyprian seemeth to affirm. But I alleged the cause why I cannot easily grant thereunto; namely, for that I see little diminished at this day of the measure which Aulus Gellius described.

36. Now it seemeth good to show the cause, why God would, that some men otherwhile should be borne of such huge stature. Augustine in the 24th chapter of the book before alleged thinketh, this was done, to the intent that it should be left for a testimony unto us, that neither the beautifulness of the body, nor the largeness of stature, nor yet the strength of the flesh should be accounted among the principal good things, seeing those are sometimes common, as well to the wicked, as to the godly. Certainly, they which bend their mind unto godliness, will judge that spiritual good things must be preferred far above; partly because they further us unto salvation, and partly because they in very deed make us better than other men. But that giants were nothing at all furthered unto salvation, through the greatness of their stature, he proveth by that which the prophet Baruch writeth in the third chapter; What is become of those famous giants, that were so great of bodies, and so worthy men of war? Those hath not the Lord chosen, neither hath he given them the way of knowledge: therefore were they destroyed, because they had no wisdom. But if a man will peruse the history of the Bible, he shall scarcely find, that they at any time took a good or godly cause in hand; nay rather he shall perceive, that through their pride and frowardness they were perpetual enemies unto God. For so was Og the king of Basan; so was Goliath and his brethren, they were most injurious to the people, whom God had embraced, and chosen from others to be peculiar unto himself.

Also there is another matter, which may very much confirm our faith. For the holy histories always make mention, that such huge giants were foully vanquished in battles; and that especially by weak men, and by men very unexpert in warfare: namely, by David, being as yet a shepherd; and by the people of Israel, when as yet they were young soldiers and ignorant in wars. Wherefore the spirit of God warneth us to be of a constant and steadfast mind, when for godliness sake we are to fight with such monstrous men. We must not then be dismayed for lack of strength, seeing the holy oracles in every place pronounce, that it is God which delivereth such huge bodies into the hands of those, whom he will defend. Which things being so, then this undoubtedly is brought to pass, that we are not in any wise to stand in fear of tyrants, (which always for the most part are against God, and have a confidence in their own great strength) when they defend a wicked cause, and assure themselves of ability to overthrow the weak and feeble flock of Christ, at their own pleasure. For against them the strength of God's word, and the power of the spirit, although we be weak and feeble of nature, shall make us mighty and invincible. Indeed in man's reason we being compared with them, may easily appear to be but worms or grasshoppers; but we being fortified and walled in by the power of God, shall not only overcome them; but (as Paul to the Romans saith) We shall conquer them. For Christ himself shall be present with us, who bindeth that strong armed man, and plucketh from him by force those most rich spoils, which he had heaped together.

Happily did he wrestle with the devil and his members; and through him shall we also fight prosperous battles, and shall obtain a far more noble victory, than the poets feigned their gods to carry with them against the Cyclops, Titans, and other the giants, which at a place called Phlaegra (as they fable) were quite extinguished by Jupiter's thunder-claps. It is proof enough, why in old time the giants, and now at this day the mightiest princes, and wise men of the world resist God: verily even because they trust and lean overmuch to their own strength, wherein they having more affiance than is meet, there is no mischief, but they dare attempt, there is nothing that they think not lawful for them. But God vouchsafeth not by such men to bring to perfection those things, which he hath determined to do; but is wont rather by David's, and such other abjects, to perform the things that he hath purposed to do; to the intent that his strength and power may far and largely appear.

37. I would think that enough hath been spoken of this matter, but that yet there remaineth a certain place to be expounded: to wit, how it is written in Deuteronomy, that Og the king of Basan was only left of the giants. What Rabbi Selomoh fableth I am not ignorant, but his exposition is so childish and ridiculous, as I am ashamed to rehearse it. Wherefore I judge that it was not spoken absolutely, and without exception, that he was left; as though there had been no giants left in the world besides himself; but it is showed, that he only did remain in those places; namely on the other side of Jordan. Further, it must be known, that not the Israelites only did rid the giants out of those regions: for the Moabites also (as we read in the second chapt. of Deuteronomy) drove them out of their coasts. Which thing also we must think did happen unto them by the favor of God: for it is there declared, that God gave those regions to the Moabites to dwell in.

CHAPTER THREE

OF THE PROVIDENCE OF GOD; UPON GENESIS 28:16.

The Grecians call providence "πρόνοια" (pronoia), or "φροντίς" (frontis). The Hebrews derive it from the verb Hisgiah, in the conjugation Hiphil, which is To see exactly and to discern. As touching the definition thereof Cicero saith in his book De inventione, that it is that, whereby anything to come is foreseen before it come to pass. Howbeit, this definition, if it be referred unto divine providence, doth not express it: because this doth only show the knowledge of that which is to come, and the power of foreknowing. But in divine providence, is not only comprehended the knowledge of the mind of God, but also his will and election, whereby things are decreed and determined to come to pass, rather by one way than another. Further, there is also a power and ableness therein, to govern and direct those things which it is said to foresee; for in things, there is not only found the nature and substance of them; but also the order wherewith they be knit one with another. And the one so reacheth to the other, that it helpeth it, or is made perfect by it: and both ways things be well ordained; particularly, as touching themselves, each of them are said to be good; and generally, as touching order, excellent good. And that this order is in all things, we may prove it by the nature of order itself: for it is defined by Augustine to be the disposition of things like and unlike, attributing to everyone that which belongeth unto it. But no man is ignorant, that the parts of the world are diverse, and not alike, if they be compared one with another.

Moreover, how conveniently each one of them is allotted by God to his own place, proper seat, and standing, both experience teacheth, and the holy scriptures testify. For it is said; That God hath set the seas and the waters their bounds, neither may they pass the limits appointed unto them. Further; He measureth the air with his span, &c. And seeing that so great a benefit of his, ought to be ascribed unto him, in respect of his providence, we may thus define it; that It is the mean which God useth in directing of things to their proper ends. In which definition is not only comprehended the knowledge, but also the will and power of doing it. Whereupon this that we avouch, Paul in the first chapter to the Ephesians, hath very well expressed, when he saith; Who worketh all things according to the counsel of his will. And Cicero in his oration for Milo, taught by what tokens this providence may be known from natural reason: for thus he writeth; Neither doubtless can any man judge otherwise, unless it be such a one, as thinketh that there is no heavenly power, nor divine majesty; and whom neither the sun, neither the motions of the heavens and signs thereof, neither yet the order and course of all things do move; and so forth. The very self-same demonstration Paul describeth in the first chapter to the Romans. And Job in the twelfth chapter; Ask the cattle, and the fowls of the air, the fishes of the sea, and the plants of the earth, and they shall inform thee. Also in the 19th psalm; The heavens declare the power of God. Again Job in the 39th and 40th chapters; Concerning the goats, the harts, the horse, the Leviathan, and Behemoth.

2. Wherefore let it thus be determined; the order of things declare, that these things which be created, are not made by chance, and at all adventures; wherefore God worketh according to his purpose: and unto his own providence, as unto a certain general and chief art, all things are subject; neither is there anything to be found, that can escape the same. Which nevertheless some are bold to deny, who think that only the chief and principal things are committed to the care of God: but the residue, if they be of small account, they attribute to natural causes; if they be of greater importance, to angels and devils. Which thing a man may see in the dialogue of Plato called Protagoras, where the creation of things is so described, that some things are granted to Epimetheus to make, and some things to Prometheus. Yet to the intent that mankind might be well provided for, this only is avouched, that it was done by the works of the gods. But in the Gospel we be otherwise taught by Christ; All the hears of your head are numbered. And; Of two sparrows not one of them lighteth upon the ground without the will of your heavenly father. Again; The Lord himself hath looked down from heaven upon the children of men. But if these men would understand the matter thus, as though the providence of God extended not itself unto all things, after such a sort as it doth unto men: we would grant it; not that the providence which is merely simple in itself, should be said to be manifold; but because the effects which be directed by it, are diverse and sundry, therefore it self also seemeth to have diverse respects. Wherefore we grant, that the providence over godly men surmounteth so far, as in comparison

of them, it is said by the Lord unto them that shall be damned, and to the foolish virgins; I know you not, and so is it over men more than over unreasonable creatures. And by a lively faith of this providence, we reap many commodities, and especially a comfort in adversity; where we know that those things happen unto us, not by casualty, but by the will and procurement of God our father. Also we be daily stirred up the more unto good things, when we understand that God is both the knower and witness of our actions; who afterward will give a true judgment of them. Besides this, the gifts which we enjoy, be much more acceptable unto us in this respect, that they be offered us by God which provided them. Further, in the same we behold predestination, which bringeth so great a comfort unto godly men, as thereby they are wonderfully confirmed.

3. Neither must we stand in any fear, that there is any newness in God, because of his providence. Men, which by their parents are brought forth into the world without knowledge, cannot attain thereunto without alteration. Which thing we must not surmise as touching God, seeing he hath had his knowledge from all eternity. Further, we draw the same from the nature of things; but he hath it of himself. Wherefore James did truly write, With him there is no variableness, nor shadowing by turning. Neither cometh it to pass at any time, that the knowledge of God is changed by the alteration of things. Moreover, this excellent knowledge is safely placed in God: for there is no danger, least he should abuse the same as men do, of whom Jeremiah in his fourth chapter writeth; They are wise only, to the intent they may do evil. But God is most excellent, and he hath the knowledge of that thing that is most excellent, which knowledge who so ever hath, cannot use other things amiss, as Plato taught in his second dialogue called Alcibiades; where it is proved, that without that knowledge, it is better to be ignorant of many things. For it had been much better for Orestes, if he had not known his mother when

he met her, being determined for to kill her. Neither is God, by reason of this government of things, removed from his peaceable felicity, or from the contemplation of better things. This thing happeneth unto men, that sometimes by dealing in matters not necessary, be drawn away from weighty and better occupations. Wherefore Paul, not without cause, condemned vain and curious questions. And this cometh through the slenderness of our understanding, which is not able to apply itself to more things at once. But God being infinite as touching all his doings, can easily perceive all things that now be, that shall be, and that at any time have been. Neither is God by this knowledge of things provoked to evil: for that happeneth unto men, because they have a corrupt desire.

Wherefore Solomon said; Behold not the wine when it showeth fair in the glass, &c. Psalm 119. Turn away mine eyes least they behold vanity. And Job in the 31st chapter, saith, that He made a covenant with his eyes, least he should think upon a virgin. But God, which is the principal rule of justice and goodness, cannot be moved to evil. But Averroes said, that at the least-wise his understanding should be embased, if he would look upon and acknowledge all these simple things. But because he atteineth this knowledge, not from the things, but from himself; therefore that is not granted, neither doth it in very deed follow. Even as we see that a glass is not therefore stained, because it showeth the images of vile things; neither yet is this sun that we see, defiled, when it shineth upon places that be foul and loathsome. Labor also in understanding doth not disquiet God, seeing in this action he useth no instrument of a body; as men do, unto whom, by means of their body, there ariseth labor in understanding, for therein the body is very much afflicted and wearied. Wherefore Solomon upon just cause, called this endeavor of knowledge, A consuming and affliction of the spirit: for knowledge sometime breedeth unto us disquietness. For the more men do understand, the more things they see that do displease them, wherewith they are aggrieved. Wherefore not without cause it is said; He that addeth knowledge, increaseth labor also. For we do not easily bear those things that be unworthily committed. But God is not subject to these human affections, who hath it in him to fore-see the end of things: and although the things be unworthy, yet he directeth them, and knoweth that they shall tend to his own glory.

4. But it hath been no hard matter, to take away from divine providence, those objections, which we have hitherto removed: for a plain and ready way was offered for the confuting of them. But there remain certain other things, more hard to be expounded. The first is, because of chance and fortune, which seemeth to be taken away from the nature of things, if we attribute unto God the providence of all: for there is nothing more against fortune and chance, than is reason. For fortune is a cause that worketh besides the purpose, when anything, not intended, or appointed, or decreed, happeneth to us unawares, and besides our expectation. But this argument we resist on this wise; As touching us, fortune and chance are not taken away by the providence of God. For what doth let (as touching God) that nothing is done by chance, but (as touching us) that many things be done rashly and by fortune? There is brought a meetly fit similitude: Admit that a master send his servant to the market, there to remain till nine of the clock; which hour being not yet past, if he send thither some other servant of his; as touching the master it cometh not to pass rashly or by chance, that those two servants meet together, seeing he fore-seeth the sending unto that place: but unto them it cometh not to pass of purpose, seeing the one knew nothing at all of the others coming. Wherefore many things, which are done by the fore-sight and knowledge of God, if thou respect the dull and weak cogitation of man, happen by chance and fortune. But if all things (say they) be directed by God, and done by his counsel, as we

believe they be, where shall now be the chance of things? For all things will come to pass of necessity. And some think this argument to be so strong against the providence of God, as scarcely the freedom of our will can be defended. But to this reason is applied in a manner the same form of answer, which a little before we used as touching things that happen by fortune. For it may be, that if thou respect the next causes, those things that do happen, both are, and are justly called things happening by chance; for it is nothing repugnant to that cause, that it bring forth as well this effect, as another effect that is contrary thereunto. For as touching mine own will, it may so come to pass, that I do sit, as also that I do not sit. So then if these effects be referred unto that cause, they shall be, by chance; for they may be otherwise: howbeit, as they be subject to the providence of God, we must not deny but that they are of necessity. Wherefore there is granted a double necessity; that is to wit, a necessity absolute, and a necessity by supposition. But it may be, that those things which by supposition are of necessity, if thou take them without supposition, they be things contingent, and not of necessity.

Isaiah in the 14th chapter showeth, that the kingdom of Babylon should be destroyed; which was but a chance, as touching the worldly causes thereof: for there was no let, but that it might otherwise be. And yet nevertheless, the prophet minding to show that it should undoubtedly come to pass, groundeth his reason upon the determinate will of God, and said; God hath so purposed, and who shall be able to disannul it? The hand of the Lord is now stretched forth, and who shall pluck it back? Wherefore the thing now by this reason was of necessity. And in the 33rd Psalm we read; But the counsel of the Lord endureth forever, and the purposes of his heart from generation to generation. Yet they still urge the contrary; Necessity seemeth to be a let to the providence of God: for we consult not of those things which cannot otherwise be.

Forsomuch then as there be many things in the world, which seem to be of necessity, those that be of this sort seem to exclude the providence of God. But here we must understand in this place, that although all things, as they have relation to the purpose and determinate will of God, being as it were done and decreed, be of necessity; yet as concerning God, the appointer and decreer of the act, all things are contingent; and nothing is of such necessity in the world, but that the same may otherwise be. Neither do we now speak of the definitions of things, or of necessary propositions or conclusions; seeing these things are not governed by divine providence: for they be descriptions of the eternal truth and divine nature. Some there be also which think, that there should be no evil found in the world, if it were governed of God by his providence. For none that dealeth providently in his works, would permit evil to take place. But these may be easily answered, that there is no evil to be found, that is not either profitable to the saints, and furthereth them to salvation; or that declareth not the justice and mercy of God; or else that advanceth not the order of all things, and the preservation of the same.

The same place is expounded in 1. Sam. 10:2.

5. But to follow some order herein; first let us search whether there be any providence, or no; secondly, what it is; thirdly, whether all things be subject unto it; fourthly, whether it can be changed; and lastly, whether it may abide any casualty of things. But before I come to the purpose, let us speak somewhat as touching the signification of the names thereof. Wherefore among the Grecians, a thing that cometh by chance is called "τύχη" (tychē), which is of such sort, as both it may be, and it may not be: and whether it be or be not, there is no absurdity, either against reason, or against the word of God. It is distinguished into 3 parts; of which the first is called by the Grecians "ἀδιάφορον" (adiaphoron), because it inclineth equally as much one way as another. The second "εἰκός" (eikos), which

for the most part useth to happen after this manner or after that, but yet may otherwise come to pass. The third is called "σπάνιον" (spanion), because it falleth out but seldom, and not usually. The philosophers assign two grounds or beginnings of chance, one in the matter, the which as it lighteth upon diverse and sundry active causes, so it receiveth a diverse and sundry form; the other in the will, whereby our actions are governed: now the will hath consideration of the matter, because it is directed and forced by the understanding. Augustine in his book of questions, quest. 31. saith, Wisdom is by the philosophers divided into three parts; namely, into understanding, memory, and providence: and that memory is referred unto things past, understanding to things present; and that he is provident, which through the consideration of things past, and things present, can determine what will afterward come to pass. But God, not only understandeth and seeth what will come to pass, but he also addeth a will unto the same. For we affirm not only a bare understanding to be in God, but an effectual will also, whereby he ruleth and governeth all things. This of the Grecians is called <H&G>, that is, Providence. And Cicero in his book De natura deorum, nameth it An old soothsaying wife of the Stoics; who was of such account among them in old time, as in the Isle of Delos, she was worshipped even for a Goddess, because she helped Latona at her child-bearing. But that fable signifieth nothing else, but that second causes, although they have some force in themselves, yet they bring nothing to pass without the providence of God. For Latona, is nature; and providence the midwife: so that unless this latter be present, do help, and as it were play the midwifes part, the other bringeth forth nothing.

6. But now, as touching those five points, which at the beginning I determined to entreat of severally. In the first place, I propound to myself, that there is a providence: which thing may be proved by many

sure and invincible arguments. For first, seeing that God is the author and creator of all things, and that he can do nothing unadvisedly, but that with himself he hath his own certain and assured reasons, therefore of necessity there is a providence. For if there be no artificer, but that he seeth the reasons and ends of his work, and conceiveth the ways by which he may bring the same to his purposed ends; it were a madness not to attribute that unto God the chief workman, whom the holy scriptures not only teach to be the creator of all things, but as it were a potter. Chrysostom in the 19th Homily upon the epistle to the Ephesians saith, that If a ship, though it be sound and well rigged, cannot brook the seas without a good master or governor; how much less can the whole workmanship of the world stand without the care and government of God? For if a master-workman will not begin to build, before he have devised in his mind all the parts, fashions, and forms of the building; shall we think, that God hath rashly, without counsel, or reason, made all things universally? Undoubtedly, the heavenly spheres, the stars, the firmament, the air, the water, the heat, the cold, so many causes and changes of things contrary and repugnant one to another, would fall to ruin, unless they were sustained by some governor. Without care and providence, our body might not be defended from the rigor of the heaven. We call those provident men, which being of such excellent judgment and disposition, do keep all the parts of their body in their proper office and duty. But God hath the same place in the world, that the mind hath in man. Besides this, the holy scriptures ascribe unto God the destructions of kingdoms, and prophesies, and miracles, which things do far pass the compass of our nature. And last of all, they attribute unto him the general judgment, wherein God will one day render to every man according to their works. Wherefore we, being induced by these, and many more reasons, do conclude that there is a providence. For we pass not for the Epicureans, whose manner of speech is this;

> Even so the powers on high,
> With labors toile are pressed,
> The care whereof which on them lie,
> Bereave them of their rest.

And this also; God walketh upon the poles of heaven, and considereth not the affairs of men. These monstrous opinions have they bred, partly for that they being of gross wit, could not perceive higher things; and partly being of a shameful and abominable life, would devise for themselves this consolation, least they should be perpetually tormented with the fear of punishments. For, He that liveth wickedly, abhorreth the light. And children, when they have done a fault, would not have either their father to be at home, or the master in the school. And as touching the first part, these things undoubtedly should be sufficient for Christians, who are persuaded only by the word of God, without other reason, that there is a providence.

7. But what providence is, we shall easily understand by the definition of the same. Providence is the power of God, whereby he directeth all things, and bringeth them to their [appointed] ends. In this definition, the general word is power. Assuredly, God is most absolute, yet for our capacity sake, we say that there is in him two manner of powers, to wit, the power of understanding, and the power of willing. For God understandeth and seeth all things; and not this only, but he also willeth all things. Here I will make no needles disputation, whether the will of God be before the understanding, or understanding before the will. If any man would know these things, I send them unto Scotus and Thomas.

This power and faculty which I speak of, belongeth unto the quality, for it is a natural power. The difference is, that God by this power directeth all things, whatsoever either be, or hereafter shall be. But yet this is not enough; for he also conducteth them to their ends. But to what ends? Even unto agreeable ends. And those be agreeable, which his purpose hath appointed. The power is the cause: and, that things be brought to their proper ends, is the effect. Here have we comprehended all the kinds of causes which can be assigned in this matter. This I speak, because there can be given no efficient cause of the providence of God. The formal cause is the power of God. The matter whereabout, are all manner of things whatsoever; for we in no wise except anything. But the final cause is, that all things may attain to their own ends, and may redound to the glory of God. By this definition we see, that the providence of God is not only a bare knowledge, but it is some bringing to effect. For as Paul saith; In him we live, we move, and have our being. And again; Of him, and in him, and by him are all things. And as Solomon saith; Man may prepare his heart, but God ordereth the speech. For we are not able to move, no not the tongue, being the lightest part of the body, without the providence of God. And Christ saith; that A sparrow doth not light upon the ground without the will of our heavenly Father. And, All the hears of our head are numbered. Some dream that God indeed made all these things; but after he had made them, cast them off. So (forsooth) carpenters, when they have done sufficiently in building of a house, they afterward leave the same: but if God should do so, this world would soon come to ruin. For a house, unless it be oftentimes repaired and underpropped, falleth to ruin and decay. If the soul be severed from the body, what remaineth, but that the body will become putrefied and rotten?

Neither are they to be heard, which say; that God indeed ruleth all things: but that this is nothing else, but to minister unto all things the common influence, which everything draweth unto itself. This is even to make God, not in very deed, but in name to be the ruler and governor of the world. For if so be that everything, according to the nature thereof do bend and apply unto itself that common influence of God, then God followeth the nature of things created; whereas rather contrariwise all things created ought to follow and seek after God. But they say, that even as he, which throweth a stone, or shooteth an arrow, hath done enough to have first forced the same, although he himself afterward follow not after them, when they be out of his hand: so it was sufficient for God, in that he endued all things with a certain power, although he do not perpetually govern them. But these things be not alike; for a stone and an arrow do fall immediately after that they be shot, because that force which is in things created cannot be of long continuance. Wherefore, unless that God should prosecute by his everlasting care and providence, the thing which he hath forced, the nature of everything could not abide. When the Peripatetiks perceived that all these inferior things, were continually troubled; they judged that the providence of God was above the moon: as if it were not convenient for it to be careful for these inferior things, no further forth than a certain common influence is thereby ministered unto all things. But these are fond reasons; for the scriptures teach us, that even these things, which to us may seem to come most of all by chance, are yet governed by the providence of God. In Deuteronomy the 19th. If an ax flying by chance out of his hands that heweth wood, strike a man and kill him as he passeth by; It is I (saith the Lord) that delivered him into the hand of the slayer. And in the 14th chapter of Job, it is said of God; Thou hast appointed man his bounds, which he shall not pass. Also in the book of wisdom, (which book though it be not in the canon, yet containeth it many good and godly sayings) in that book (I say) in the eighth chapter, it is written; Wisdom reacheth from one end to another "μηκος" (mēkos), and disposeth all things "σωφρόνως" (sōphronōs): it reacheth (saith he) "κραταιως" (krataiōs), that is to say, Strong and mighty: and disposeth Profitably: for so soundeth "σωφρόνως" (sōphronōs); and not Sweetly, as the old translation hath. And that profit, although it be not oftentimes perceived of us, yet is it always of such sort, as it doth tend to the glory of God.

8. But whether all things be subject to the providence of God, is a matter in controversy: for some say, they be; and some say, they be not. But, as we said before; if God have made all things, undoubtedly nothing is exempted from his providence: for if anything should be exempted from his providence, that also should be exempted from creation. It is written in the epistle to the Hebrews; He upholdeth all things by the word of his power. The Hebrew phrase; The word of his power is instead of His mighty word. This place agreeth with that which we cited out of the book of wisdom. Ezekiel calleth God; The Lord of all flesh. And Moses calleth God; The Lord of spirits. And Paul saith; It is he that worketh all things, according to the determination of his will. Also Hesiodus an Ethnic poet saith; In this life we can nowhere escape from the mind of God. Yet there be some which would exempt from God's providence, men and free will, and things that either be of necessity, or that come by chance. Cicero in his book De fato saith; that The most ancient philosophers, such as Empedocles and Heraclitus, affirmed, that All things come to pass of necessity: but the Peripatetikes were of the opinion, that many things come by chance. And Chrysippus as a notable umpire, although he taught that all other things were of necessity; yet affirmed, that man's will, as touching the first election, is free. Wherefore Eusebius in his treatise De praeparatione evangelica, said pleasantly, that

Democritus made men to be slaves; but that Chrysippus made them but half slaves.

Also Cicero in his second book De divinatione, will rather exclude all providence, than that men should not be free. Which vanity Augustine deriding in his fifth book De civitate Dei, saith, that He to make men free, had made them rob God of his glory. So we see, that there be some which think not, that all things be under providence: but in that they except man by name, which is the chiefest workmanship of God, that seemeth too contumelious a thing against God. For seeing all artificers contemn trifling works of small value, but do adorn, and have a special care of those works which be excellent; who will imagine that God could despise that work, which of all other he made most choice of? And if it should be so, in what state stand we? What refuge should we have in adversity? David saith; Cast all thy care upon God, and he will nourish thee. And Peter saith, It is he that taketh care of you. And Zechariah; He that toucheth you, shall touch the apple of mine eye. And I (saith the Lord) am thy buckler, and thy strong wall. The Lord (saith David) is my helper, and I shall not be afraid what man can do against me. Though their tents were pitched against me, yet my heart shall not be afraid.

9. But thou wilt say, that In inferior matters, many things are done either without order, or else disorderly: for we see often-times the godly to be oppressed, and the wicked to flourish. Admit it be so; but is there no providence therefore, because we do not see the causes thereof? If peradventure thou shouldest be in a smiths shop, and seest many tools, some crooked, some bowed, some hooked, and some sawed in; wouldest thou strait-way condemn them all for naught, because they appear not straight and handsome? I think not; but thou wouldest rather confess thyself to be ignorant of the use of them. Such an honor must be given to God, as when thou seest tyrants and wicked men to enjoy wealth and

prosperity, thou must say, that they be instruments of the providence of God, although thou canst not perceive what God intendeth by them. Augustine saith, that God is so good, as he is able to draw out some goodness even out of the wicked. Further, if there were no tyrants, what virtue and patience of martyrs should there be? God will have some to be the triumph of his goodness, he will have some also upon whom he may exercise his might and power. But perhaps thou wilt say; Is it not enough that men be martyrs in the preparation of their mind? Indeed there be noble virtues hidden in the minds of the godly, but yet oftentimes this doth not satisfy God: he will bring them forth into act, that they may be seen. Wherefore our eyes must be lifted up, that we think not of the ungodly, but of God. So the prophets call Nebuchadnezzar, Pharaoh, and Sennacherib, hatchets, hammers, saws, and swords in the hand of God.

Job, when he was turned out of all that he had, respected not the Chaldeans, nor the devil, but said; The Lord gave, and the Lord hath taken away. He is accounted a learned physician, which can draw out unto the outward part of the body the corrupt humors, which be hidden within the body; yet we would abhor blanes and sores: but the physician saith, that then the sick man beginneth to heal, when such things break forth. In like manner God, with his medicines and fires of persecutions bringeth into light those things, which before lay hidden in our minds. Let the wicked do what they will, yet can they do nothing more than is the will of God. So said Peter in the Acts as touching Pilate and Herod; They agreed together, that they might do, whatsoever thy will and thy counsel had decreed to do.

10. But thou wilt say; Some things be of necessity, which cannot otherwise be than they are; do those fall under the providence of God? Yea truly, there is nothing created of such necessity, but if it be referred unto

God, it hath the nature of a thing that cometh by chance. For as we said; God reacheth from end to end, and ordereth all things. What thing is of more necessity than the course of the sun? And yet Joshua made the sun to stand still. What thing is of more necessity, than that the fire should burn, if fuel be applied thereunto? Therefore it hath been an old saying; If active things be applied to things passive, the action must follow of necessity. Yet nevertheless God brought to pass, that those three young men walked safely in the flaming furnace. What is of more necessity, than that the shadow should follow the sun shining? And yet God brought to pass, that when the sun did shine, the shadow went backward. But man seemed to have been made, and to be left in the hand of his own counsel. Thou shalt keep those things (saith Ecclesiasticus) and they shall keep thee. I grant that man, as concerning the inward causes, was so made at the beginning, as nothing could be to him of any necessity: but we do not therefore exclude the grace of God and providence. Let us hear the holy scriptures as touching that matter. For Ecclesiasticus is not among the number of the canonical books; The kings heart (saith Solomon) is in the hand of God. But God saith; I have given them precepts. But he also saith; I will make you to walk in my commandments. Again; I will give you a new heart, and a new spirit. Wherefore man is not to be exempted from the providence of God.

11. But much less are those things to be excluded, which seem to be done by chance. For although we cannot perceive the reason of the second causes, yet God seeth it; yea, the Philosophers teach us, that every cause, which they call Per accidens, that is, Coming by chance, must be revoked unto that which is a cause by itself: for that which is Per accidens, cannot be any cause. Wherefore Aristotle in his little book De bona fortuna, when he demanded for what cause some were fortunate, and some not? He answered, that it is done by a certain violent motion,

and impulsion; whereof nevertheless, he that is driven, cannot yield a cause: hereby it cometh to pass (saith he) that some are fortunate, and some not. Furthermore he saith, that this event, if it be referred to our will and knowledge, happeneth by chance; but that enforcement is a cause by itself. But the question is not thus dissolved. For how cometh it to pass, that this fortune is given to one man, and not to another? The Astrologers would supply that, which they thought Aristotle wanted. Ptolemy in his book <H&G>, referreth this unto the stars; by which (he saith) men being diversely borne, are carried some to prosperity, and some to adversity. And this, some called, A power, some Constellation, and other some Particular destiny; Socrates called it Daemoniu. But why it happeneth more to one man, than to another; and more at one time, than at another; none other cause can be assigned, but the providence of God: which undoubtedly is, that all things should be referred to the glory of God.

It is not you (saith Joseph to his brethren) that sold me into Egypt; but God sent me hither before you. So God said that he sent Saul unto Samuel, although it seemed as if he had turned out of the way to him by chance. So Christ said unto his Apostles; There shall one meet you bearing a pitcher of water. These things were certain unto the providence of God, although otherwise in the sight of men, they might seem but things coming by chance. But thou wilt say; Be there then no second causes? Doeth God nothing by his angels? We take not away the second causes; but we make them instruments of the providence of God: for Angels be administering spirits. And David saith; Who do execute his will. But although God send his angels, yet he himself is present and principal over all things; If I shall ascend (saith David) into heaven, thou art there; if I go down into hell, thou art there also. For he doth not so give his angels charge, as though he himself were absent. Which thing the poets feign of Apollo, that he placed Phaethon in his chariot, and by that means all the heavens in his absence were set on fire. But sins, (will some man say) depend not on providence. How sins be ruled by God, shall be showed afterward. In the meantime this I say; The cause of sin undoubtedly cometh from us: but at what time, and against whom it should break forth, that is in the power of God. It was wholly determined by Nebuchadnezzar, that he would oppress some people; but that he should oppress the Jews more than others, that was provided by God.

12. The next question is, Whether this providence be immutable. Why should it not? For it is the rule of all things that be done. It is written in the third of Malachi; I am the Lord, and am not changed. In the first of James; With him there is no variableness, nor shadowing by turning. And in the 19th of Proverbs; There be many cogitations in the heart of man, but the counsel of the Lord continueth steadfast. In the 46th of Isaiah; It is I that speak, and my counsel abideth surly, and I do what so ever pleaseth me. For seeing providence is both the knowledge and will of God, and that those things belong to the very essence of God, it cannot be changed, except God himself be changed therewithal. The second causes indeed, seeing they be diverse and sundry, they oftentimes hinder themselves; which thing we see come to pass in the influences of heaven, that some of them be an impediment to others; but the will of God cannot be hindered by any violence. In old time God ordained the ceremonies of the Jews, afterward he would have them to be abrogated. How then? Is not the providence of God mutable? I answer; that In God is altogether one and the self-same will; but that he fore-saw from the beginning, what might agree with the diversity of times. Augustine to Marcellinus saith, that A husbandman doth sometime sow, sometime reap, and sometime compass the soil; yet we must not say that the art of husbandry is therefore mutable. Vindicianus saith, that A certain

physician ministered a medicine to a sick man, and healed him; and that he many years after falling into the same disease, took the same medicine without the counsel of the physician: but when he waxed worse, he came to the physician, showing him the matter, and began to complain of the medicine. No marvel (quoteth Vindicianus) then; for I ministered not the same unto thee. Now when some men marveled thereat, and were of opinion that he used some enchantment; There is no such matter (saith he) for now is he of another age, and hath other humors than he had when I gave him that his medicine. But shall not therefore the art of physic be like itself? Even so in any wise God, although he foresee all things, yet he hath not decreed, that all things should be done at one time.

13. Now let us come to chance. If so be that the providence of God be so certain, whether can it admit any casualty? Here will I first use two distinctions, and afterward I will answer. There is one necessity which is absolute, and another conditional. For when we say, that God is wise or just, we understand that that is simply, and absolutely necessary. There be other things necessary by supposition; as that which is commonly canvassed in the schools, to wit, that whatsoever is, while it is, is necessary. Christ and the prophets fore-showed that the city of Jerusalem should be overthrown; therefore of necessity it shall be overthrown: not that this necessity is in the nature of the city, but because Christ and the prophets have foretold it, who could not be deceived. Paul saith; that There must needs be heresies: and Christ saith; It is necessary that offenses come. For these causes being set down; namely, the corrupt natures of men, and the devils hatred towards mankind: and the end being granted, to wit that the elect should be tried, it is necessary by supposition, that it should so come to pass. Also things may be considered two manner of ways, either as they be in act; and in that case they have the nature of

necessity, for they be no longer indefinite. As, to write, or not to write, is by chance: but if thou be now in the act of writing, it is no more chance, but necessary. Wherefore we say that the knowledge of the senses is certain, because the things themselves cannot otherwise be. Or else things may be considered, as they lie hidden in their causes: but seeing causes may sometime bring forth effects, and sometimes not, therefore there is no necessary power of working in them. But if those things be referred unto God, the reason is far otherwise: For he calleth those things which be not, as though they were; for he comprehendeth all time, and hath neither beginning nor ending. All things also, which are to come forever hereafter, are notwithstanding present unto him. Here also cometh in the will of God; for we must not ascribe unto him a bare knowledge; but such as is effectual, or actual. And by this means I say, that the very things themselves are to be considered as necessary. Augustine In genesi ad literam, the sixth book, chapter 15. There be many ways whereby man, and other things might have been made by God, and those means had some possibility, and no necessity: but this is by the will of God, whose will is the necessity of things. And though such things, being referred unto God, be necessary; yet of us they must be weighed according to their inward and proper causes, and so be called things contingent, or that come by chance. For it is of no necessity, that such as the efficient cause is, such also should be the effect.

14. If thou demand, Why these two kinds of causes be in the nature of things, so as some be limited and necessary, others indefinite and contingent? Nothing else can be answered, but that God hath laid these conditions upon all things. God bringeth forth all things, and he limiteth and boundeth all things; but yet so, as he neither confoundeth nor destroyeth the nature of things. Boetius in his Topics saith, that Destiny is so called, of drawing to, and giving place fitly: for God draweth all

things; but yet after a sort so giveth place, as he disturbeth nothing. Even so things, although in their own nature they incline indifferently on both parts; yet by God, they are made to incline more to one side than to another. The will of Saul, of his own nature, was no more determined to go than to tarry: but when God would send him unto Samuel, that will began to incline to the one part. And therefore God put into his mind the will of his father, and brought to pass, that the same should effectually move and persuade his mind: and that all other desires of rest and ease (if any were) that might have retained him at home, should be subdued. Wherefore it came to pass, that the will of Saul obeyed the providence of God. But yet in the meantime, the nature of the thing was not violated; but that the will of Saul was alike free unto either part. Hereby it appeareth, how necessary the grace of God is unto us. For our own will, as it is all manner of ways corrupted, turneth all things to the worser part. Also there be many things, which do dull and blind our understanding, that the will cannot easily follow. God therefore propoundeth good unto our understanding, afterward he kindleth faith, and stirreth up the will that we do will the same effectually.

15. But thou wilt say; Why is anything said to be contingent, seeing God hath already determined of the one part, and so it is made a thing of necessity? I answer; Every thing of his own property and beginning is contingent; but providence, which bringeth a necessity, is an outward cause, of which nothing ought to be named. I know there be many, which affirm, that those things which cannot be done by man's power, are brought unto that pass by God, that our will may either choose or refuse them; and that there the providence of God stayeth, and goeth no further: but when as God foreseeth what every man will choose, and what he will refuse, his foreknowledge hindereth nothing at all. Howbeit, these sayings do not sufficiently agree with the holy scriptures.

For they teach, that God doth not provide for things, that he will forsake them; but that (as we have said) he may conduct them to their ends, and those ends do serve the providence of God. For so saith Paul; God hath made all things according to the purpose of his will. So said God himself in Isaiah; All things that I will, I do. And Christ saith; Verily, even a little sparrow lighteth not upon the ground without the will of our father. I know that Origin, Cyril, Chrysostom, and others being urged by certain manifest places of the scriptures, such as these are; It behooved Christ to suffer; The scriptures ought to be fulfilled, do thus interpret them; to wit, that these things did not therefore come to pass, because God fore-saw them; but therefore God fore-saw them, because they should come to pass. This judgment of theirs, if they spake as touching absolute knowledge, could not much be reprehended. For, not because I see a man writing, therefore he writeth; but because he writeth, therefore I see him writing. Howbeit, we cannot affirm a bare knowledge in God, but we must also attribute unto him a will, whereby he directeth and ordereth all things. Yet shall it be true that they say, if their meaning be of the effect, or (as they say) A posteriore, that is, of the latter. For we hereof, that a thing is done, do understand, that it was the purpose of God that so it should be. Otherwise the scriptures speak very plainly; It behooved Christ to die; It behooved that the scriptures should be fulfilled. But how did it behoove? By supposition; because God so for-saw it: not that that necessity was in the nature of the thing.

16. But peradventure thou wilt say, that therefore the causes in the nature of the thing it self be infinite, for that I take not the perfect and full causes, in so much as I should have added the providence of God. I answer; I only take the inward and proper causes of everything, whose effects, because they might or might not be brought forth by them, be things contingent. But I add not providence, because the same is an

outward cause. The which being added, it cannot be avoided, but that by supposition, some necessity must follow. For, Saul met with men caring of kids, bread, and wine: their will, in respect of the nature thereof, was infinite, either to have given him, or not to have given him anything: but God by his providence did limit that will unto the one part. They went to Bethel, there to sacrifice; they met with Saul weary upon the way, and almost dead with hunger; it seemed a courtesy to refresh him: this did God put into their minds. And if there were anything, which might be a let unto this will, those things he bridled. And these things we dispute only concerning the wills of men: for otherwise, in other things which be contingent, I know the means be infinite, which God is wont to use. Another example of this matter we have out of the 21st chapter of Ezekiel; Nebuchadnezzar marched into Syria, and when he was now onward on the way, at a place where two ways met, he began to consult with himself, whether it were better for him to lead his power against the Jews, or else against Rabath the chief city of the Ammonits. He drew lots thereupon, the lots did God so frame, that he brought him to Jerusalem. The nature of the thing itself was contingent, but the same being appointed of God became a thing of necessity. Joseph was so sold and carried into Egypt, that as concerning the nature of the thing, it might be, that either he should live always in bondage, or else that he should at one time or other be delivered. But God sent dreams into the Baker and Butler; those dreams did Joseph interpret: afterward he showed Pharaoh a dream, which when none of the diviners could expound, the Butler gave him intelligence of Joseph: and by this means it came to pass, that Joseph was delivered out of prison. Wherefore be it thus determined (as we have said) that all things having relation to the providence of God, be necessary; but of their own nature are contingent.

But thou wilt say; Shall the affects be absolutely called things coming by chance, or rather of necessity? Some there be, that for the dignity of providence, will have them called necessary: but I would rather call them contingent, according to their own nature. Albeit I will not greatly strive, so that the same necessity be understood only by supposition. Rightly did some of the Greeks name providence "διοίκησις" (dioikēsis), of passing through; because it passeth through everything: others called it "πρόνοια" (pronoia), because nothing can escape it. Some will say, that we receive the opinion of the Stoics concerning destiny. That is not true; for they defined their destiny to be a necessity by a knitting together of causes, and affirmed that the same did over-rule even God himself. But contrariwise, we teach that God governeth all things, and that he useth them to his own glory. But if they affirm that destiny is nothing else, but the providence of God; the question is only as touching the word, and not of the thing: as Augustine else-where hath taught. Lastly, thou wilt say, that by this means, there will be no place for advisements, admonitions, and corrections, seeing that which God will, must needs come to pass. The self same thing was objected to Augustine, where-upon he wrote the book De correptione and gratia. Undoubtedly God, although he have decreed a thing to be done, yet he useth means in bringing the same to pass. He will change the naughty will of man; he useth admonitions, preachings, and chastisements. For these be the instruments of God's providence: so far is it that the providence of God excludeth them. In this question we have set in a manner the roots, and laid the foundations of predestination: but of it we will entreat another time, when opportunity shall serve.

I know I am misreported, that I make God to be the author of sin; but that is not true, as it shall plainly appear. But I only endeavor by my doctrine, to show how the scriptures must be understood, when they seem so to affirm: Also what Augustine meant, who said, that God bendeth the wills of men as well unto good, as unto evil: And in like manner, how Zwingli and Oecolampadius, and other great learned men, professors of the Gospel, must be understood, when they seem to avouch the same.

CHAPTER FOUR

WHETHER GOD BE THE AUTHOR OF SIN; OUT OF 2 SAM. 16:22.

L ook in Jud. 3:9. and 9:24. and 2 Sam. 2:27, and 1 Kings. 22:21. and in Rom. 1:23.

It remaineth now, that we entreat of the question; Whether God be the author of sin? For as well the curse of Semei, as the defiling of David's concubines, may seem at the first view to proceed from God. For as touching the curse, David himself said, that it came from God. And as touching the adultery of David's concubines, it was spoken by Nathan under the person of God. Wherefore it may very well be called in controversy, whether God be the author of sin. And truly there are very many and strong arguments of both sides: a good part of them I will recite, unto the which all the rest may be referred. [1] God cannot truly and rightly be said to be the cause of sin. Excellent is the sentence of Augustine, in his book of 83 questions; God is not the author of anything, whereby a man becometh the worse: But no man doubteth that men are the worse through sin, Therefore God cannot properly be called the author of sin. It is not likely, that God will deform man: artificers desire to adorn their works. [2] Further, God himself generally in the scripture professeth himself a revenger of sins. If he be a revenger, he is no author; for then he should punish his own. If he were truly the cause of sin, he should condemn that which he made, which thing is absurd. [3] Thirdly it is said, that He loveth those things which he made, and hateth nothing that he hath made. But he testifieth that he did hate sin, therefore he doth not enforce to sin. To hate and to love are contrary; wherefore both cannot be spoken of one thing, at one and the self-same time. If he hate sin, then he loveth it not; but if so be it were of God, it should be beloved: for God loveth those things which he made. [4] If God were the cause of sin, he in the bringing forth of sin, should sin; he that stealeth, is a thief; he that committeth murder, is a man-killer: but far be it from God, that he should be either said to sin, or to be a sinner. What is else to sin, but to stray from the right end? But God is infinite, and cannot be lead away from the end by another greater force. He is not ignorant, that he can stray from the end; for he is most wise. And that he himself should cause others to sin, it seemeth to be absurd.

[5] Let us consider what is done among these natural things created by God. There be many efficient causes; it seemeth that every efficient cause coveteth to make that like unto itself, whereabout it worketh. Fire, if it take hold upon wood, so worketh, as those things, whereupon it worketh, may be made like unto itself; a man doth procreate a man. Thus in things created do agents work; why shall we not say, that in God's doings, his endeavor is to make like unto himself; and that therefore he sinneth not? The holy scriptures teach us the same; they bring in laws

which stir up good works, but sins at no time. [6] If God should provoke sin, or would it to be done, he should seem to be a hypocrite; he should closely and secretly do another thing, then he openly pretendeth. [7] Jeremiah spake of false prophets; They ran, but I sent them not; they prophesied, and I spake not with them; namely, that they should speak this thing. [8] Oseas saith; Thy salvation, O Israel, is of me, thy perdition is of thyself. But no man is ignorant that sin is the cause of perdition. If perdition were of Israel, then sin also: but salvation, and whatsoever goeth before salvation, is of God. If salvation and perdition, being the effects, be thus distinguished; the causes also must be distinguished, the one to be of God, and the other of man. Sin shall proceed of men, and virtues of God. [9] More manifest is that which is written in the eight chapter of John, where Christ speaking of the devil, saith; When he speaketh lies, he speaketh of his own: if of his own, he hath no need to be stirred up of another. [10] And again, This is the condemnation of man, that light came into the world, but they loved darkness more. [11] James testifieth, that God tempteth no man. But by temptation, men are provoked unto sin: wherefore if God were the cause of sin, it might not be said, that he tempteth not any man. It is concupiscence whereby we be tempted, and that is not of God, but of the world.

2. [12] In the second of Paralipomenon, the last chapter, there is a special place, where the cause of the destruction of Jerusalem is given and ascribed to the sins of the people: and in such sort it is so disproved, that God is the author of sin, as God testifieth that he would it otherwise: wherefore the cause must not be laid upon God. He sent his prophets (saith he) betimes in the morning, but they hardened their heart. [13] Christ wept over the city of Jerusalem; he was sorry for the overthrow thereof. If the effect displeased him, much rather did the cause: he wept, because they so sinned, as they deserved utter destruction. If Christ wept,

who not only was man, but very God also, he was displeased with sins: therefore God is not the author of sin. [14] Neither can it be affirmed, that God is the cause of sin, unless we will charge him with tyranny, in that he condemneth men for their sins, because they have done wickedly, whom yet after a sort he hath led unto wickedness. Tyrants are wont to set forth laws, and then to provide cunningly that their subjects may commit something against those laws, whereby they may punish them. [15] Moreover, the scripture attributeth unto God the judgment over all flesh: but how shall he judge the world of sin, if he himself have been the author of sin? In the third chapter to the Romans; If our righteousness do set forth the righteousness of God, is God unjust for punishing? That it may be perceived how absurd a thing it is, that our sins should make to the glory of God: for if they make to the glory of God, why doth he condemn them? If the reason be there of force, it more strongly concludeth in this place. If God be the cause of sin, how shall he judge the world? [16] Also there will seem to be in him two wills, and those one contrary to the other: but in God there is only one will; if there should be more, they would be one against another, as touching one and the self-same thing; so that he would have us both not to do, and to do the self-same things. [17] We will demand, to what purpose are so many exhortations, persuasions, and callings to do well, in the holy scriptures? All these things will seem to be vain. To what end did Christ give warning unto Judas, if he would be betrayed of him? These speeches may seem to be done as it were in game. But God dealeth gravely and earnestly in those things, which he dealeth with men. [18] Also there would follow a great absurdity; for the differences between good and evil, and between virtue and sin, would be taken away. God should be appointed the author of both; whereas he being the sovereign good, there can proceed nothing but goodness from him. If a man should detest murder, adultery, and

incest, he would say; it is a good work. The matter would be brought
to such a pass, as good would be called evil, and evil good: yea rather
there would be no difference at all betwixt them. For through the will
of God, whereby he forbiddeth and commandeth anything, we judge of
good and evil: but by this means we should be void of all judgment.

[19] In like manner would be taken away the judgments of our consciences. We read in the epistle to the Romans, that we have cogitations,
which shall defend and accuse one another in the judgment of the Lord.
If this other opinion were true, we will gather, that we should not accuse
ourselves, but God the author. [20] There is plenty of excuse for the
wicked, they will say; Wherefore need I to repent for this thing, seeing
God himself is the author of it? Repentance will be taken away, and
a window opened unto great mischiefs. [21] Wherefore shall we give
thanks unto God, because he hath delivered us from our sins? But sin
was good; It had been all one to have lien still in sin; [22] We will not
lament our sins, but rather rejoice in them, for it is the work of God; it
is meet that we should rejoice for the works of God. If God himself be
the author of sin, praise and rejoicing will follow; but not sorrow. [23]
Much will be drawn away from the estimation of God, if he should be
put the author of sin. [24] That saying also, which they show, might be
brought; namely, that God would have all men to be saved. If he will have
them to be saved, he useth good means; he encourageth not men to sin:
for sins do lead men to perdition. Many more reasons might be brought,
but for this time we will content ourselves with these.

3. Let us see on the other part, what things they be that might affirm
God to be the cause of sin. [1] In the first chapter to the Romans it
is written; that Seeing the idolaters knew God, and would not worship
him as God, therefore (as meet it was) he gave them up unto a reprobate
sense, and unto shameful lusts. If he gave them, he also provoked and

moved them. [2] In Exodus it is written, that God had hardened and dulled the heart of Pharaoh, so that he would not hearken, when Moses commanded him in the name of God to let the people depart. [3] In the sixth of Isaiah, He is said to blind the people, that they should not see. [4] When we pour out our prayers before God, we desire him that he Lead us not into temptation, but that he will deliver us from evil. To what end should we thus pray, if these things should not sometimes be? No man entreateth, except for those things which may be, or which do hang over his head, or which he feareth will come to pass. They are wont to say, that God doth and willeth these things, not as they be sins, but in respect that they be punishments to chasten him that hath sinned. But it is hard to appoint the punishment and fault to be all one thing, seeing the nature of punishment and fault is diverse. A fault ariseth from the will, whereas punishment is laid upon us against our will. If it be committed voluntarily, then it is no punishment. To affirm a thing to be voluntary, and yet unvoluntary, can hardly be made to agree. [5] That, which is the cause of a cause, may also be called the cause of the effect: but no man doubteth but that God hath given us a will, inclinations, properties and effects, whereby we are provoked to sin. If God be said to be the cause of these things, why dare we not say that he is the cause of sins? [6] That which removeth the impediments, if the thing afterward happen, or the effect follow, it shall be called the cause of sin. What doth chiefly let sins? Even grace, and the good spirit of God: except these keep us back, we shall rush headlong into most grievous crimes. Who can remove grace, or take away the spirit, but only God which gave them? If he remove the lets, no doubt but he is some cause of sins. [7] Also, he that ministereth an occasion of anything, he seemeth to be an author thereof: although he be not the chiefest cause, if he give an occasion he shall not fail to be called author. God knew the hardness of Pharaoh's heart, and he knew that he being not holpen by the spirit, would be provoked to sin. So The law is said to increase sin, if it be not proposed to the regenerate: for we always bend ourselves unto that which we be forbidden, and covet that which we be denied. God commandeth [Pharaoh] to let the people go; what is this, but to offer an occasion that he might be the more hardened? We cannot deny but that God doth minister occasions: yea, and he not only giveth occasions, but we can also show commandments wherein he commandeth sin. [8] We have in the history of the kings, that Ahab was a wicked prince; that God determined to punish him in battle; he would have him brought to this by the flatteries and false persuasions of false prophets. God is brought in to talk with the spirits; Who can seduce Ahab? There stepped forth an evil spirit which said; I will be a lying spirit in the mouth of the false prophets. God alloweth and commandeth it; Go thy ways, do so. He giveth encouragement; It shall be so.

[9] Further, we cannot deny, but that sin is a certain human action: but every deed, as it comes in act, dependeth of the first principle of all things. God is (as the Philosophers acknowledge him) Primus actus, the first agent. Unless he be the upholder, there can be no agent: wherefore sin dependeth on God, as upon the cause efficient. [10] Sins for the most part be motions; and motions have an order, so as the inferior dependeth upon the superior: therefore the cause of sin, so far-forth as it is a motion, is directed unto his own mover. [11] Augustine hath certain testimonies of this thing, and confirmeth it also by some places of the scripture. In his book De gratia and libero arbitrio, the twelfth chapter, he saith; that There is no doubt, but that God worketh in men's minds, to make their wills incline, either to good according to his mercy, or unto evil according to their merits; by his judgment undoubtedly which sometime is open, sometime secret, but evermore just. In the beginning of that chapter he saith; Who can but tremble at these horrible

judgments of God, whereby he worketh what he will in the hearts of the wicked, yielding to everyone according to his deserts? And he addeth; He verily worketh in the hearts of men the motions of their will, and by them he doth those things that he will do, who nevertheless cannot will anything unjustly. This he proveth by the scriptures. In the first of Kings we have the history of Roboam, who hearkened not to the counsel of the ancients, that he should deal mildly with the people. But it is said, that this turning away was of the Lord, to the intent he might establish the saying of Ahia the Silonite. Wherefore (as Augustine expoundeth it) that naughty will was of the Lord. He alledgeth another place, out of the second book of Chronicles, the 21st chapter. God stirred up the Philistines and Arabians against Joram, which followed idolatry; God was minded to punish him. Undoubtedly the motions of the minds in the Philistines and Arabians were wicked against Joram, insomuch as they invaded other men's countries, and were infected with cruelty; and yet God is said to have stirred them up. In the same history of kings, there is speaking of Amasias, which provoked Joash the king of Israel unto battle. Yea and Joash himself, and also the prophet of the Lord discouraged him from the purpose; but he being carried with ambition, hearkened not unto the godly admonitions: which thing nevertheless came from God, who would that he should be delivered into his hands, because he followed the idols of Edom.

4. [12] We read in the 14. chapter of Ezekiel; If the prophet be deceived, I have seduced him; and I will stretch forth my hand, and will smite him. He entreateth of the false prophets, which ever between whiles vainly fed the people. [13] Jeremiah saith in the fourth chapter, that God deceived the people. [14] In the 63. chapter of Isaiah the prophet complaineth; Wherefore hath God so seduced the people, or made them to err, that they should depart from him? [15] Solomon

saith in his Proverbs; Even as the violence of waters, so is the kings heart in the hand of God. Undoubtedly Pharaoh was a king, therefore he inclined his will unto what part he would. [16] Nebuchadnezzar was a king, therefore he inclined his will unto which part he would. [17] In the 104th psalm, it is said of the Egyptians, that God turned their hearts, so as they hated the children of Israel: they seemed before to love the Israelites. [18] In the second epistle to the Thessalonians, the second chapter; Because men cast away the love of the truth, therefore God sent them strong illusions, that they might give credit unto lies. It is written in the eleventh chapter of Joshua, that None made peace with the children of Israel, among all the nations of the Chanaanites, save only the Gabeonites. For God encouraged their heart to fight against the Israelites. And it is added, unto what end; namely, that they should be weeded out by them. Assuredly, he did animate them, that they should not desire to have peace, but rather to have war. [19] Moreover, he that would an end, seemeth to will those things, which serve unto the end; and by the same will he would those means which crave an end. The physician, willing to heal a sick man, seeth that cutting, or searing, or else a bitter potion is fit, and even these he will use for recovery of health. When God would that a testimony unto the truth should be given by the martyrs, and that Christ should die, he also would those things that should procure this end; namely, the vexation of the saints, and cruelty of kings and people: for it behooved to attain unto that end by these kind of means. [20] In the prophets, especially in Isaiah, kings are said to be in the hand of God, like rods, hammers, and axes; which comparisons have no place, if it were not understood, that God moveth the harts: for they be not moved, unless they be driven forward. [21] Also when God was displeased with the people of Israel, he stirred up the heart of David to number that people by the poll; which thing was wicked. It is to small purpose, if thou wilt say that in the book of Chronicles is read, that Satan provoked him: for Satan can do no more than God giveth him leave. Whether God did it by himself, or by Satan, thou seest that David was stirred up by the will of God, unto that which was not lawful. They are wont to excuse this matter, that God permitteth, but not helpeth. We say, it is not enough; for the offense is still left in our minds. [22] God as yet seemeth after some sort to will sin; he knoweth, that a man cannot stand by himself. If some blind man should walk before us, and we should see him ready either to stumble against a stone, or to fall into a ditch; and we are present, we may help him, but we will not, we suffer him to go on: now when he falleth, shall not we after some sort be said to be guilty of his fall? For thou wouldest have him fall, if thou diddest not stay him when thou mightest.

[23] And that which yet is more grievous; if so be that an old impotent man were leaning upon his staff, and so after a sort were going, and if some man should take away his staff whereunto he leaned, although he enforced him not to fall, should he not after some sort be called the author of the fall? God taketh away his spirit from weak men, who without this be not able to go; doth he not after some sort seem to be the cause of their fall? Wherefore, that which they bring, will be a weak defense, when they say that God forsaketh men. [24] While we would seem to excuse God, we lay as grievous things unto him; to wit, that he is no more a God; and while we shun the smoke, we fall into the fire. If any things be done besides the will of God, whether he will or no; if there be any effects, whereof he is not the cause: he is not then the universal cause of all, nor yet God. But he compelleth not to fall; the excuse will not serve. [25] Admit there be some good man of the house, whose family behaveth itself very ill: if he be reproved, he will excuse himself, saying; I bad them not, I commanded them not: that excuse shall not be counted lawful; for

he ought not to permit that which he could have hindered. Many times the good man of the house cannot let wicked acts, but the power of God is invincible. There be no wills so evil and corrupt, but he can amend and make them good. [26] Anselmus in his book De casu diaboli, the 91st chapter; Why (saith he) do we account it absurd, that God doth particular actions by a naughty will, seeing we know, that he maketh sundry substances, which are brought forth by an dishonest action? As when a child is procreated by adultery. [27] That adultery is evil, no man doubteth, but that child is the creature of God. This seemeth twice to be affirmed in the Acts of the apostles. In the second chapter Peter saith of Jesus the son of God; that The Jews had taken him, and delivered him to be slain by the determinate will and counsel of God. Afterward in the fourth chapter, when the church gave thanks unto God, it prayeth on this wise; Against thy holy son Jesus, both Herod and Pontius Pilate, with the gentiles and people of Israel, gathered themselves together, to do those things that thy hand and thy counsel had determined to be done. With these arguments, whereunto others might be added, I will hold myself content.

5. Now that we have set down the reasons for each part, there remaineth that the question itself be expounded. I find three opinions; the first is to be detested, namely of the Libertines, which say, that God is all wholly the cause of sin: and so say, as they affirm, all sins to be excusable, and not to be reproved, because they be the works of God: and if any fault should be, they would lay it upon God. This one thing they endeavor; namely, to take away from all men the feeling of sin. If any man have committed murder, it is not he (say they) that hath committed it, God hath done it. And unless that a man so think, they say, that he is imperfect, and cannot allow of all God's works. What can be more wickedly imagined? The devil could not have found out a readier way to

hell. Let these men go to perdition, seeing we cannot mend them: let us pray unto God that he will take away these pestilent persons out of the church. The second opinion is of certain learned men, who mislike not that sense, which the scriptures appear to have at the first sight. They say, that God hardeneth, that he punisheth sins with sins; and finally, they grant him to be the cause of sin: but they add, that these actions, seeing they proceed from the very corrupt nature of men, so far forth as they be of God, have a respect to justice; and that men be not excused, because they be inclined unto these things: they lay not the blame unto God, who doth his part rightly. If (say they) it cannot be comprehended by reason, how he doth justly, and we unjustly; we must refer ourselves to the judgment of the scriptures. There be many other things, which by man's reason we cannot know, which nevertheless we do believe. The third opinion is of them, which interpret all these places of the scripture by the words; He suffered, He gave leave, He permitted, or according to the Greek; He did not hinder it, and such like. So they think that all dangers are avoided.

6. But what my judgment is, I will not be loath to declare; afterward your own selves shall judge. And that the matter may be the more easily known, it shall be good to examine it the more deeply: and somewhat I will say, of Evil, under which general word, sin is contained. Evil is a certain privation, of good I mean; yet not of every good, but of such a good thing as is requisite for the perfection of every creature, which I say belongeth to the perfection of the thing despoiled. For if we take away sight from a stone, it shall have no hurt: for that quality of nature is not meet for it. Evil being a privation, cannot consist without good: for it must have a subject. A subject seeing it is a substance, is a good thing; wherefore evil cannot be but in good: even as blindness is a privation of sight, it hangeth not in the air, but it sticketh in the eye. So may it

be showed by many other examples. But not to depart from that which we have in hand; sin itself depriveth man's action of dutifulness and obedience towards the word of God. These things ought to be in action; but when we sin, action is bereft of those good things. And action, seeing it is a certain thing, it is in his own nature good; wherefore evil cannot be but in good. Moreover, evil is not desired for itself, but men do sin in consideration of good; for unless there appeared some likeness of good, they would not depart from goodness. So great therefore is the power of good, as evil cannot be except in good, and unto good. Wherefore rightly have the wise men said, that we may grant, there is the chiefest good; but not affirm that there is the chiefest evil, which can deprive good altogether: for then it should destroy it self. It might have no subject wherein it should be, nor yet outward show, whereby it should be desired. To speak now of evil; it is distinguished into punishment, and fault. Fault is called that which we commit against the law of God; punishment is that which is laid upon us for sin: and that also hath a privation of some commodity; as when God sendeth sickness, sickness is the privation of health, and hath place in the body of a living creature. He sendeth famine and bareness, which is the privation of fertility; and it is in the earth itself: this (I say) belongeth unto punishment. But sin taketh place in the mind only: punishments doubtless may both be in the mind, and in the body. There is added a third member, which is so a punishment, as it is also sin: as original sin is, so is the natural corruption left after baptism. These things thus concluded, I put forth a certain sentence or proposition to be confirmed, the which hath two parts. The first is, that God is not by himself and properly the cause of sin. The second is, that there is nothing done in the world, no not sins themselves, without his will, determination, and providence.

7. To prove the question, it behooveth to confirm it as touching both parts. Let us speak of the first; that God by himself is not the cause of sin. Unto this purpose serve the arguments in the first place. But I add, that when good or evil are opposed, as Habit and Privation; the habit by itself doth never bring in privation. Light itself doth always illuminate, it never bringeth in darkness. Wherefore if we put good and evil as contrary privatives, evil shall not be of good. God is the chiefest good, let us then put him to be the habit: wherefore by himself and properly, he maketh no privation. But I said that he is not the cause of sin by himself and properly. These words I have added, because, if we will speak less properly, he may be said after some sort to be either the beginning, or the cause of sin: not indeed the proper cause; but that cause, which of the philosophers is called removing or prohibiting. I will make the matter plain by similitudes. The sun is altogether bright, the proper effect thereof is to make light; yet after some manner it may be said to make darkness, not in that it shineth, but in that it is moved, and departeth from one place to another. For bodies be round, therefore when it departeth, it cannot always by reason of the motion, give light to that place from whence it went, but shadows do come between: so then after some sort it is said to make darkness by the departure thereof; because bodies are so ordered, and it self is moved.

So likewise it happeneth as touching some ruinous house; it is held up by a prop, some man approaching removeth the prop, the stones and buildings through their own weight fall down from the top; which things have in themselves the causes of their coming down: yet notwithstanding, he which taketh away the prop, is said after a sort to cause the fall: for he removeth the stay which letted the ruin. In like manner God, in his own nature is good, yet in respect that he is just, he will punish sinners; he taketh away his grace, and after some sort may be called the cause of those things which afterward be naughtily done; yet not the true cause: for that proper cause is inward, that is to wit, the naughty will of them. But why he sometimes taketh away his spirit from men, a reason may be yielded; when they sin, he removeth his grace from them, not only to the intent he may punish, but that the excellency of his favor may be known: and to let us understand, that that which God giveth, he giveth it freely, and that it is not of nature. For if we should always have [his grace] and after one and the self-same manner, as if God would not at some time stack his strength, we would attribute unto our own power the good things that we do. But thus it is, to the intent we may acknowledge our own infirmity, and pray the more fervently for preservation and increase of the heavenly gift. But when the grace and favor of God is justly taken away from us, sin doth naturally follow: neither is there need of any other efficient cause; I mean, there needeth no other cause, to come from our infected and corrupt affections.

This appeareth by the similitudes alleged, if the sun be removed, darkness doth follow; not through any efficient cause, but by itself. If the habit be removed, privation is straightway present of his own accord. If one so hurteth his eye, as the sight be lost; blindness doth immediately follow: neither is it needful to seek any other thing that worketh. Which seeing the Manichees perceived not, they erred most shamefully: they would not attribute the cause of evil unto the good God; but they saw that there were many evils, and they judged that evils could not be without a true cause: whereupon they affirmed that there be two beginnings. And because they saw a great power to be both in evil, and in good, they brought in two gods; one good, and another bad. Of these we read much in Augustine. But that evil, which is sin, cometh, if the spirit of God be taken away: for then man is left unto himself. But whether is he so left, as God doth no more anything concerning him, or his sin? That this may be understood, I will declare three sorts of working, which we may perceive in God towards his creatures: not that other works of his cannot be showed, but because these three do most of all serve unto the matter we have in hand.

8. Some action of God is general, seeing by his providence he cherisheth, sustaineth, and governeth all things in their conditions, qualities, and inclinations, as they stood at the beginning when they were created. And thus is the order of nature preserved; which thing is excellent to be known. We see that heaven retaineth his own nature: surly it hath many things to be marveled at. We see that the nature of fire is vehement, of air is pleasant, of water is flowing: we see also the metals, the trees, the works of artificers, which things assuredly be wonderful. All these are governed by God; yea, and if he should withdraw his hand from them, they would fall to nothing. Profitable doubtless is the consideration of his divine government. Oftentimes doth God exhort us in the psalms, to magnify him for these works. In the first to the Romans it is written, that The Gentiles by these creatures did know God, and a kind of his everlasting force, working, government, and godhead, in such sort, as Aratus said; We are in very deed the linage of God. We have an excellent example of this work in our selves. The soul which is not seen, is indivisible, yet it moveth and quickeneth the whole body. Even so all creatures do retain their properties and inclinations.

9. Secondly, another work of God is, whereby the creatures are not only preserved and ruled, but do also obey the counsels of God. For God useth the actions of all things, even of men, and of evil men: he useth them (I say) for the establishment of his purposes. When he favoreth his own, he giveth them plentiful increase of fruits; the rain falleth early and late. But if he will of his justice punish the wicked, nothing cometh well to pass; there is given a heaven of brass, and an earth of iron: if the

fruits be ripe, they perish in one night. These things must not be ascribed unto fortune. When we know not the cause, we take it to be fortune; whereupon the poet saith,

A goddess Fortune we thee call,

And place thee high in heavenly stall.

Wherefore we must not occupy ourselves alonely in a general consideration of things of the world, but we must weigh the use wherein they serve the providence of God; whereas sin cometh of proper causes, I mean of our own will, and corrupt affections, yet doth the same serve God also. A similitude; There be many poisons in the world, they have many and dangerous qualities; yet the physician occupieth them, and the magistrate rightly useth them. The physician by tempering of the poisons, healeth the sick: the magistrate at Athens gave poison for the taking away of such as were guilty. So was Socrates compelled to drink hemlock. Although therefore poisons are evil, yet may the magistrate and the physician use them well for the safety of the common-wealth, and preservation of the sick. Even so God ruleth sins (which have their proper causes corrupted) for the performing and bringing forth of his counsels to act. I might also use another similitude; Those things which seem to be done of us by chance in the world, do most of all serve the providence of God. For the Lord saith in the law, Exodus 21, and Deut. 19. If two shall go together into the grove to hew wood, and the axe flieth out of one of their hands, and he is smitten therewith that stood next him, and is slain: this he did unwittingly, he shall not be guilty of death. For God delivered him [thereunto] and that for just causes delivered he him of a determinate purpose; we understand it not, he knoweth it. Even so they which offend, indeed they do as they would, they have determined with themselves what they will do: but yet God useth these actions. So by the curse of Semei, God would have the patience of David to be thoroughly known unto all men, and would open his judgments against his adultery and murder: but this man meant to show his hatred against David. God doth that which he will, as touching those crimes which men of another purpose committed; not to the intent they might obey the will of God, but their own corrupt lusts.

And to return to the testimony now alleged. He that heweth wood, this he would do, but the axe hitteth another man, and the hitting serveth the counsel of God. Jerome upon the twelfth chapter of Jeremiah writeth, that Nothing happeneth rashly and without providence, whether it be good or evil; but that all things come to pass by the judgment of God. Wherefore creatures be certain instruments in the hand of God; he useth them according to his own purpose. But yet these instruments be not all after one sort; for some there be which have no knowledge, nor sense, nor will, and yet nevertheless they do service unto God. But there be others, which perceive, understand, and will those things which they do, and yet they do it not always of purpose to serve God: yea rather they oftentimes unwillingly and unwittingly do that which God appointeth. Wherefore we will say, that as well living creatures, as not living creatures; things having sense, and having no sense; Angels good and bad, and generally all creatures be the instruments of God, which he useth according to the consideration of his providence. He did use the Assyrians, Chaldeans, Persians, Greeks and Romans, for punishment of the wicked Hebrews: he did use also the devil against Saul and against Job. But it is further to be considered, that when God useth creatures, especially the reasonable creatures, and evil creatures, such as be evil men and devils; he doth not so use them, as though they did nothing themselves; for even they themselves fulfill their own naughtiness, but God useth it [to purpose.] God dealeth not with these as with stones, which have no sense at all; they will, they know, and they have sense: and when wicked men, and the devil do naughtily, and are moved by their own proper lust, they do service unto the providence of God. They perceive doubtless, and will, not that their mind is such as they would serve God, for they seek their own. Neither are they so moved by the superior cause, as they use not withal their own naughtiness.

10. But thou wilt say, that If God after this manner, have recourse as the chiefest cause unto these actions, and that evil men as the next causes do them, it shall be all one work of God, of the devil, and of naughty men. This indeed must not be denied; but yet this work cometh far otherwise from the superior good cause, than from the next cause which is corrupt. This work, as it is of the devil, and of wicked men, is evil. It draweth infection from the wickedness of the devil, and of naughty men; which being evil trees, cannot bring forth good fruit. But God, the very best, and chiefest cause, as he concurreth with these actions, doth them rightly and in due order. Even as both God and the devil would Jerusalem to be destroyed, but yet in sundry respects; God, to the intent he might punish the obstinate; the devil, that he might fulfill his cruel hatred against mankind. Christ was to be delivered unto the cross, which also was done; and this work, as it proceeded from the hatred and malice of the Jews, was evil: but the self-same, in as much as God, through that most holy action, would have mercy upon mankind, had goodness. Wherefore it is said in the Acts of the apostles; that They did those things against the Son of God, which his counsel and hand had determined. Yet must those things which they did against Christ, merely be called evil; because they have both their name and nature from the next cause, although that God rightly used them according to his own providence. The devil and God exercise Job in a far sundry respect; also the Sabees, and other robbers spoiled his substance for the satisfying of their own hatred: so did the devil. But God did it to prove his patience, and to testify his good will

towards the godly, by a joyful deliverance. Wherefore the works were all one, but the purposes were diverse. For which cause, when Job said (The Lord hath given, and the Lord hath taken away) he praiseth God, as the chiefest cause, without whose providence these things were not done, and whose providence used all things to a good end; yet doth he not praise the robbers, and the devil. So did David also behave himself; he commended not Semei, he said not that those cursing's were of their own nature good: but turned himself to the providence of God. The work was wicked, yet in some respect it may be called the work of God; because he ruled it and used it. Also it is said in the prophet; Cursed be he that doth the work of the Lord negligently: and the work of the Lord he calleth the affliction of the people, whereby the wicked overpressed them. Wherefore, the wicked cannot excuse their sins, in respect of this use of God: for they have the cause of those sins in themselves. And even as God's good use of these things excuseth not sinners, so on the other part, the naughtiness of sinners doth not contaminate the good use and providence of God, who can exceedingly well use the things which be done amiss.

Augustine in his Enchiridion ad Laurentium, chapter 101 declareth, that It may be, that God and man would one and the same thing; and that God in so willing, doth rightly; but that man doth sin, although he will those things which God willeth. He bringeth an example. The father of a wicked son sickeneth, the will of God by his just judgment is, that he should die of that disease, the ungracious child also would the same; but to the intent he may the sooner come unto the inheritance, and be free from the power of his father: God willeth justly, but the child ungodly. And on the other side (he saith) that It may be, that a man would the thing that God would not, and yet that as well he as God willeth rightly. Admit that the father, which is sick, have a good child;

God would that the father should die: the child thorough an honest affection would it not, for he is desirous to have his father live; they will diversely, and yet they both will justly. It consisteth only in the purpose of the will; for thereof dependeth oftentimes goodness and naughtiness. But there ariseth a doubt; If that one manner of work depend both on God and man, and that it draw naughtiness from the infection of man, and that it hath some goodness, in respect that God useth it, so as nothing may escape God or his providence, wherefor doth Zechariah in the first chapter complain; I was but a little angry with my people, but they helped forward unto evil; that is, they passed the bounds. That which they sin, seemeth to exceed the providence of God; so as they did more than God had decreed. We answer, that It must not be understood, that they did more, than that thing might serve to the use of God's providence: for there can be nothing at all done besides the will of God and his decrees, which be most firm. Augustine in the same Enchiridion ad Laurentium, 102nd chapter, saith; The will of God is invincible, how then are they said to have exceeded? Not the bounds of the eternal decree, but the just measure of victory. There be certain bounds, limits, and laws, which ought to be kept by conquerors. They exceeded that which became them, but that they could do more than providence would use, it must in no wise be granted.

11. The third kind of the works of God we call that which is proper unto the saints; for thereby he most mercifully bringeth many things to pass in them: for he reigneth, he liveth, and he worketh in us both to will and to perform. Otherwise in nature we be certain barren trees, we are blind, we will no good things. The judgment is corrupted, the will and choice is corrupt in those dregs of original sin: but God, by his spirit, fashioneth his chosen anew. We have from the beginning a nature given according to the similitude of God, whereunto should be agreeable, to

will, to choose, to do these things and those things. But in that we cannot do good of ourselves, it hath proceeded of corruption: but in that we will rightly, and do serve God by an obedience begun, it is of the supernatural grace of God. Wherefore the first kind of God's works, which belongeth to the universal providence, serveth not to the question now in hand. The second kind of working and the third belong unto this.

12. Although therefore that God do govern even sins and evils; yet he is not properly said to be the efficient cause. Augustine in his twelfth book De civitate Dei, the seventh chapter, speaketh very well as concerning a naughty will, when he saith; An evil thing hath no efficient, but a deficient cause. And if any will search out this efficient cause, it is even like as if he would see the darkness with his eyes, or comprehend silence with his ears: which being privations, it is no need that they should have efficient causes. Yet nevertheless, they be things known unto us; for there is all one sense of things that be contrary. The sight seeth not other than bright things, the ear heareth not other than noises, and yet by these senses we know even these things; not by the use of them, but by the privation only. A naughty will doth God use, to the ends appointed: not because he is not able, unless it be by these means, to attain to that which he will; but so it pleased him to declare his wisdom and power, that he might show himself able to do something mediately [as they say] and immediately: and that it maketh no matter unto him, whether the instruments that he useth be good or bad. Wherefore let us seek out what is the deficient cause of evil actions, and among the rest we shall find wicked affections and inclinations, which seeing they fall away from the word of God, and from right reason, it is no marvel if things that be faulty, proceed there-from. These be the inward causes of sin, but they be rather deficient than efficient causes. The devil also is said to be the cause of sin: for we read in the book of wisdom; By the devil death entered

into the world, therefore sin also: for death is the effect of sin. But yet
the devil cannot be called the proper and absolute cause of our sin: the
reason is; for that such is the nature of every proper and perfect cause,
that the same being put, the effect doth of necessity follow. But in the
devil it is not thus; for although he sometime suggest evil things in the
mind of the godly, yet nevertheless sin doth not always follow. For many
godly men do valiantly resist him, and when sin followeth not, he cannot
be called the absolute and perfect cause thereof. In deed, he provoketh
men, but yet not so, that sin must of necessity follow.

I might bring another reason. Let us imagine that the devil himself had
not revolted from God, and that man had been created, man could yet
of his own nature have sinned, and have had the cause of sin in himself:
but the suggestion of the devil could not have been the cause thereof,
when he was not as yet alienated from God: so that he is no perfect nor
full cause of sin, but a persuading and alluring cause. We have therefore
showed from whence sin hath his deficient cause; namely, from our own
corruption. Yet nevertheless God doth govern and rule sin itself; he doth
not idly look on, but he doth the part of a judge and governor: and he
leaveth not all things without guiding. But after what sort is he said to
govern sin? Even as touching time, manner, form, and matter; to wit,
that it is carried sometimes rather against this man, and sometimes rather
against that man. Our corruptions lie hidden within us, but God suffereth not the same at all times to break forth, nor yet so long as the wicked
would: he bridleth sins, and sometimes interrupteth them. Further, he
bringeth to pass, that our wickedness shall rather bend unto one part,
than unto another; as the rage of Semei was more bent against David,
than against another man. And the providence of God is showed rather
at one time than at another; God directed the power of Nebuchadnezzar
rather against the Hebrews, than against their neighbors.

13. There is also a certain other thing to be considered of in sins, when they break forth into act. God himself putteth us in mind of some things, which in their own nature be good: and yet because such things fall into the wicked, they be taken in ill part, and be occasions of sinning; so as the sins which lay hidden before, do break forth. But yet these suggestions, either inward or outward, cannot be properly called the causes of sin, seeing those causes be within in men: yet may they be called occasions. But of occasions, some be given, and some taken; in like manner as they distinguish Scandalum, that is, an offense. An offense taken, is the occasion of an offense, not on the behalf of him that giveth it; for he doth that which is profitable, but an ill man doth ill interpret this: that is, an offense taken. So Christ saith of the Scribes and Pharisees; Let them alone, they be blind, and leaders of the blind. The apostle taught, that men ought to do well; if others were offended, the fault remained not in them. An offense given, is when we do those things which we ought not to do. But in God it is not so; he suggesteth some things, that of their own nature are good, the which falling into an evil nature, become occasions of sinning.

14. The matter must be made plain by examples. Some godly man seeth a man sin, he cometh to him, he diligently warneth him to beware: that which is put in mind is good, but it happeneth into a naughty mind, which then beginneth more and more to break forth into the hatred of virtue, and to wax cruel against the godly. This admonition was an occasion that these things should break out into act; God suggested by the godly man that which in nature is good, wherefore he is said to do rightly, for he doth that which was his part to do. But unto evil men, good things are made occasions of sinning, yea and of more grievous sinning, than if perhaps they had not been ministered. Howbeit this is the difference between God and us; that we, while we suggest good

things, are ignorant whether the party will become the worse; but God is not ignorant. For example; God sent Moses and Aaron unto Pharaoh, he commandeth that he should let his people go: this suggestion in his own nature being good, Pharaoh taketh in ill part, and began to be the more cruel. If this suggestion had fallen into a godly man, he would have said; It is meet I should obey God: and because it is his will that I should let the people go, I will in any wise do it; for I can challenge no right over them longer than he will himself. But Pharaoh, when he heard these words, began to blaspheme, saying; Who is this God? And he brake out into cruelty. The same will we declare by other examples and testimonies of the scriptures. Not only that admonition given unto Pharaoh by Moses and Aaron is a good thing, and is applied outwardly by God; and he which was evil, used the same naughtily: but we have the self-same thing in the seventh chapter to the Romans; The law is holy and spiritual, but it hath wrought in me concupiscence and death. The commandment of God in his own nature is unto life, but the filthiness [of sin] taketh an occasion by those things which are suggested. Neither is this done outwardly alone, but sometimes also God worketh it inwardly by good cogitations: for whatsoever things are good, we must always think that they be of God. Pharaoh, which came after the death of Joseph, began to cast thus in his mind; We must take heed that the common-weal suffer no detriment. This cogitation was good, and it proceeded from God; but it lighted into an evil mind, therefore it was wrested against the Hebrews: for he said; The people of the Hebrews will increase, and when occasion is offered, will subdue us: wherefore let them be destroyed. He set forth an edict, that all the men children of the Hebrews should be thrown into the river. The first cogitation was good, but through his naughtiness it turned unto evil. Nebuchadnezzar said; It is not the part of a good prince to be idle, but he must exercise the power which he hath. The cogitation was good, but he turned himself unto foreign nations, and armed not his power as he ought to have done, against the wickedness of his own people. The same prince (as we read in Daniel) being in his hall, reckoned with himself the victories which he had, and the greatness of empire which he had gotten. These thoughts were good; for we should weigh with ourselves the benefits of God, but they lighted into an evil mind: he straightway thought with himself, that he had established the kingdom by his own power: therein he sinned against God. Also the sons of Jacob weighed with themselves, that Joseph was beloved of his parents, that he had divine dreams put into him by God; this was a good thought, for we must behold the works of God even in others, much more in our own selves. If they had rightly used that cogitation, they should have given thanks to God, but they turned it to envy, they devised how to rid him away, and to sell him. Undoubtedly God, who suggesteth these good things, seeing he knoweth of the doing of them, he doth not there let the occasions of evils: he suffereth them to be done; for he is at hand with his providence, and governeth them. Wherefore by Pharaoh he would be glorified, by Nebuchadnezzar he would punish the Israelites, by the brothers selling of Joseph, he would have him to be honored with great benefits in Egypt, and to feed the household of Jacob. Semei saw David to be cast forth, and the kingdom to be given unto Absalom: he said; These be the judgments of God. That cogitation was good, it fell into an evil mind, he abused the same, he spake contumeliously against David, he followed his own wrath and revenge. Absalom having gotten the kingdom, was put in mind that he should hearken unto the counsel of the wise, that many eyes do see more than one eye. The cogitation was good, but it fell into an ill mind; and he judged that counsels, so they be profitable, though otherwise they be wicked and dishonest, should be harkened unto. The first suggestion that was good, he used naughtily:

God suffered it, he would not let it, he ruled it, that the sin of David might be punished, and that the hatred of God towards sin might be showed. Now I think that the matter is evident.

15. But it is demanded, that Seeing God knoweth that wicked men will abuse these inward and outward motions, although they be good, wherefore doth he suggest them? The reasons of his own counsels are known to himself; but yet two reasons are set before us. The first is, that his justice may appear the more: for to behold the justice of God we are blind. But by making comparison it is known; namely, by unrighteousness, whereof in God there can be none seen: but in devils and corrupt men we see it. The second is, that the boldness of men may be restrained: for many would say; If God should put into our minds good cogitations, we should have a will and power to do good things. Behold, good cogitations are given, the which, while they fall into a corrupt nature, except it be restrained, sin (through our own fault) doth arise even of things be they never so good: of occasions (I mean) taken, but not given. And so I understand the words, which Augustine hath in his book of Grace and Free-will; namely, that God doth sometime incline our wills, either unto good or unto evil; because if the things, which he suggesteth, do light upon good men, they are inclined unto good; but if they fall into ill men, they are inclined unto evil. And so I understand that which he writeth against Julianus the fifth book, and 3rd chapter; that God worketh not only in the bodies of men, but also in their minds. So likewise I understand those things which Zwingli (of godly memory) a learned and constant man, did sometimes write; that Men are other whiles by God's providence provoked to sin: and that one and the self-same action cometh both from God, and from wicked men; justly from him, and unjustly from them. And thus I understand those

places of the scriptures, wherein it is said, that God gave them up to a reprobate sense, that He stirred them up.

16. Certainly a permission is there, but something that is more ample is showed by these effectual speeches. And we grant, that there is a permission; for if God would resist, these things should not be done: therefore he permitteth; howbeit we must understand, that permission is a certain kind of will. In deed it is not the efficient will, but yet it is a kind of will. For as Augustine saith in his Enchiridion ad Laurentium; God permitteth either willingly or unwillingly: doubtless unwillingly he doth not, for that should be with grief, and there should be a power greater than himself: if it be with his will, he permitteth; permission is a certain kind of will. But thou demandest, that If he will it any way, wherefore doth he forbid it? On the other part I would demand; If he would it not at all, how cometh it to pass that it is done? For the will of God is invincible. Paul saith; Who can resist his will? God willeth, and that which he willeth, he willeth justly. They which sin, do will unjustly that which they will. That same Julianus, against whom Augustine disputeth, held, that there was a bare permission in those things; to the intent we might understand, that God doth nothing at all: and he said, that God doth rather suffer, and that this belongeth to his patience. Augustine answereth; Not only to his patience, but also to his power: because he ruleth sin, and thereof he worketh what he will. And he alledgeth a place unto the Romans; If God, willing to show his wrath, and make his power manifest, did suffer with great lenity the vessels of wrath, &c. Hereby indeed we see, that he suffereth; but that mention is also made of his power. In the first epistle of Peter the fourth chapter, it is written; Wherefore let them that suffer, according to the will of God, commit their souls unto him. So that he attributeth the afflictions of the Christians to the will of God. But they cannot suffer,

unless there be a doer. If he would the suffering, he would the doing: for suffering proceedeth from a doer. This will is a permission, but yet such as belongeth also unto the will.

This did Augustine show in his Enchiridion ad Laurentium, the 100th chapter, where he treateth upon that place of the psalm; Great are the works of God, searched out upon all the wills of them. He followeth the Greek translation. The Hebrew text hath, Unto all the will of them. He writeth; that So far as belonged to them, (he entreateth of sinners) they did that which God would not. This could they not by any means bring to pass, as touching his power: for even in this, that they did against his will, his will was wrought upon them; therefore great are the works of the Lord. He addeth, that by a marvelous and unspeakable means, even that which is done against his will, is not done without his will: for unless he suffered it, it should not be. Neither doth he suffer it unwillingly, but willingly: neither would he, being good, suffer ill to be done; but that he being almighty, of that evil, can make good. The will of God concurreth both to good things, and to evil; but after a sundry manner: to evils, indirectly: he suffereth them to be done. He suggesteth good things, but because they happen into evil men, sins do ensue. But as for the good things, he not only suggesteth them, but he bringeth them to pass. Yet he ruleth and governeth sin also, that it may not rage against every man, neither at all times, nor beyond measure. Those evils lurk within us, but when they break forth, they cannot escape the providence of God. But good things (as I have said) he not only letteth not, but he bringeth them to effect, he worketh together with us, and he sweetly bendeth our will, that we may be glad to do those things that did mislike us.

Wherefore the respect of general providence is one; the respect of using of things, though evil, is another; and the respect of things, which he doth in us that be regenerate, is another. So understand I, that Pharaoh was hardened by God, and that also he hardened himself: for he had in himself the cause of obduration. But God is said to have hardened, by reason of suggesting and governing: further, because he so ruled sin, and used the same to his own glory. And Paul saith, that he raised him up for to declare his power. So understand I the vessels of wrath to be prepared unto destruction. By what means? They be of themselves, of their own naughtiness, of their own corrupt nature prone unto sin. In like manner it may be said, that they after a sort are prepared by God; because through his good suggestions, wickedness breaketh forth: and while it breaketh forth, it is yet in the hand of God to apply the same as he will, one way or another; for God with a good will doth that, which we do with a most perverse mind. Permission is a kind of will, but yet not absolutely: for the will of God properly is the cause of things. It is not as man's will is, we will many things, which we bring not to pass. What is then the cause why God would not have sin? It is, for that sin is among those things which have no need of a cause efficient, but of a deficient cause. Therefore sin doth not properly come under the will of God. And if that God be put as the cause, not efficient but deficient, shall we say that God doth fail in himself? No; but he is said to fail, because he doth not hinder, nor resist, nor cause to relent. What manner of will shall this be? A will not to hinder, a will not to mollify, a will not to illuminate.

17. Neither for all this, doth God, either by suggesting anything, or by not letting, constrain the will; neither can the devil do this. For if the will should not work of his own accord, it were no will; but rather an unwillingness. It may as ill be ascribed unto the will to be compelled, as to the fire that it should not be hot. Wherefore our nature and will being so corrupt, if the favor of God be withdrawn; of his own accord, and by itself, it inclineth to evil. The which nevertheless, from the time of his beginning was not evil: but because it is brought forth of nothing,

and is confirmed and sustained by the grace and power of God; if that
be withdrawn which confirmeth it, straightway it will to worse of his
own accord. But if man's will be not constrained to evil, neither is evil
of his own creation, but only is said to sin by depravation; what shall we
say as touching the sin of the first man? In him nature was good, grace
and the help of God was not wanting, and yet nevertheless he sinned.
Here we say, that we must judge one thing, as concerning the first man;
and another as touching our nature, which we have now corrupted. God
bestowed upon him many gifts, but yet he so made him, as he might
stand; he might also fall. No doubt but God, if he would, might have
made him so perfect, as he could not have sinned. Which the state of the
blessed saints doth declare; for the holy spirits in the heavenly habitation,
and we when we shall be there, shall be so confirmed, as we shall not be
able to sin anymore: otherwise it would be no perfect felicity; it should
be joined with a fear of falling. But yet he did not this unto Adam; and
whereas by his prescience or foreknowledge he knew that he would fall,
he might have kept him there-from; but he would not, but would suffer
him to fall, and by his eternal decree had Christ to be the remedy of
his fall. The rest of the things concerning that state, we cannot more
particularly declare, because we have not the perfect knowledge thereof.
Let us return to our own state; the which is such, as before the renewing
by Christ, we were not able to will any good thing, but of necessity to lie
in sins, neither might we lift up our selves: so far is it off, that we should
be able to stand upright, as it was granted unto the first Adam.

But although God, as we said, is not properly the cause of sin; yet
must he not be drawn out of his throne, but that he also ruleth sins, and
maketh a remedy for them. And this we may be assured with our selves,
that there can be nothing done either of us, or of any creature, besides
the will of God. But yet let us not hereby excuse our sins, as though

we would obey the will of God by committing of sin. We must accuse ourselves, seeing we have the originals of sin in us. As concerning the will of God, we must follow that which the scripture teacheth; and we must not depart from his law. And when we otherwhile depart from him, we must weigh with our selves, that the motion of turning away from God, and of the inclination to allurements of this world, is a thing proper unto our will being now corrupted, not as it was instituted by God. Wherefore there be deficient causes of this motion; but an efficient cause which hath God a worker together with us, we must not seek. Whereupon we note in the book of Genesis, that it is not said that darkness was made of God; The darkness (saith he) were upon the face of the deep, yet God did so order them, as they should prevail by night: they were privations. So this motion of turning away from God, seeing it forsaketh, and depriveth men's actions of convenient goodness, a cause surly it hath, but the same is deficient.

18. These things being declared, there remain three things to be spoken of: the first shall be of the guiltiness of sins, or bond unto punishment: the second of the subject of deformity and privation; that is, of the act itself of man's will: the third is (which also is commonly received) that sin is the punishment of sin; and whether under these three considerations it may be said, that sin dependeth on God. As for the first, we must understand, that the deformed and naughty act, is in some respect the groundwork unto the punishment that is due; for The reward of sin (saith the Apostle) is death: and when we sin, there groweth a bond, whereby we must suffer punishment for the wickedness committed. That guiltiness is said to arise through the justice of God, in consideration that he will yield to everyone that which belongeth unto him: but the bond ariseth not, except that sin be or have been; so as by sinning we give a just occasion of the bond unto punishment.

Wherefore, if by sin we understand the guiltiness and the bond, we doubt not but these things are of God, as of the efficient cause. Howbeit, these things ought not properly to be called sin, seeing they belong unto justice, yet sometimes they are so called; as when we say, that God doth remit, blot out, and forgive our sins: for he bringeth not to pass that they be not, nor have not been (and undoubtedly there remain evil motions in us) but the bond of suffering punishment, for the wickedness committed, is taken away, which (as we have said) belongeth unto justice, and is a good thing.

19. Secondly, let us consider of the subject itself, unto which the deformity of sin doth cleave; and of this, if we speak as the thing is, we shall not be afraid to say, that God is the cause, seeing the action itself is a certain natural thing. And whatsoever is, in respect that it hath a being, is brought forth, not by creatures alone, but by God: for All things (saith the scripture) were made by him. This universal particle comprehendeth all things, whatsoever they be, by what means so ever they be, and how far forth so ever they be. Augustine in his book De moribus monachorum, about the beginning saith; that The catholic church believeth, that God is the author of all natures and substances. What he understandeth by nature, he declared a little before, by these words; Nature is nothing else, but that which is understood to be some certain thing in his kind. Wherefore as we now, by a new name, of that which is Esse, to be, do call essence, which many times also we name substance; so they in old time, which had not those names, instead of essence and substance, called it nature. Seeing therefore the motions of our minds be certain things, there is no doubt but after this manner they depend of God. God assuredly worketh as the highest cause; the creatures work together with him. Wherefore Anshelmus in his book De casu diaboli, wrote, that Even the evil willing of the devil, so farforth as it is to will, dependeth on God.

And the thing itself is not wicked, but in respect that he himself doth naughtily will it. And that the same act is something, hereby it appeareth; because it is in the general word or predicament of action: wherefore as it is something, it is of God, and is a creature. Yea and Augustine in his ninth book De trinitate, and tenth chapter, said, that The accidents of the mind are better than the accidents of the body; by reason of the worthiness of the subject. Wherefore the form or beauty, as it is in the mind, is more excellent, than as it is outwardly found in the body. Also the soul itself, being a soul, how ill soever it be, is yet more noble than any body. Seeing therefore the deeds of the mind (whereunto afterward, through our own fault, there cleaveth privation) so farforth as they be things, are not brought forth without God.

Anshelmus in the place above cited, saith, that God himself is the bringer forth of things, and that not alonely of substantial things, but also of accidental, universal, and particular things, yea, and of the evil motions of the will: for the power of God is infinite. Wherefore there is nothing can be brought forth whatsoever it be, but is under his action; for if anything could escape the same, then should it not be infinite, then should it not fill all things? Neither might our will break out into act, unless that high supreme will wrought together with us. Augustine in his treatise De vera religione, the 34th chapter, writeth thus; that The very being itself, be it never so little, is good; for the chiefest being, is the chiefest good. And a little after he saith; The chiefest beauty is the chiefest good, the least beauty is the least good, yet is it good. So as, if that action, which we speak of, do by any means pertain to the being, it is of some goodness. Wherefore, if we dispute of sin, we must distinguish it, and we must see what is therein of the positive, as they reason in the schools: and the first subject itself must be considered; and on the other part, to see what defect and privation cleaveth thereunto. But in the very same privation, since we see a defect, the deficient cause thereof must be sought, and not the efficient cause. But that which is there found positive, hath need of an efficient cause; and the sum of all efficient causes is God.

20. But here ariseth no small doubt. There be certain sins, called sins of omission [or negligence,] and there seemeth not to be grounded the very act and work of will, whereunto either defect or privation should cleave; howbeit whatsoever is there, it seemeth to be privation. A man is said to omit his duty, because he doth not that which he ought to do. As for example; If a man love not his neighbor, if one come not to the congregation to hear the word of the Lord, and to participate the sacraments; here in this sin, there seemeth only a privation to be, without any certain act, whereupon this should be grounded. Some answer, that even in this place also, we are to seek a nature or action, a work or a thing, that is the groundwork unto privation: and they say, that it is the will which maketh defect. For even that same sinning will, as it is a nature, is kept in his order by God; but not in respect that it sinneth. This saying may be borne withal. But in searching the matter more narrowly, it seemeth otherwise unto me; and I see even in those sins of omission, that there is an act. For the same omitting of our duty, is sometimes done by contemplation; and then that corrupt person hath a will not to love his neighbor, hath a will not to go to the holy assembly.

Wherefore we see here, that the act of will, and that same action thereof, which is the action of nature, doth depend of God; deformity and privation doth not so. But sometime they be omitted, because a man doth not think of those things, I mean not, of a contempt. Here, say I, that although there be no action there of that kind, yet is there another, which contendeth with right reason. He is not mindful of the holy congregation, because he will walk about for his pleasure, or else use some pastime; and those actions be adversaries to right working. Or if that be no action at that instant, yet was it a little before. For example; Overnight he would feed like a glutton, afterward he could not rise early to be present in the holy congregation. Wherefore in the sins of omission, we shall find an action, either proper to that kind; or else another striving with the good motion of the will, either which is then presently retained, or else that went before.

21. God then is the cause of all things; and inferior things, according to their own nature, receive the moving of the first cause. Wherefore, if sin be drawn, it is drawn by the nature of the second causes. I will make the matter plain by a similitude; In living creatures we have that power which hath his name local motion, and it moveth beasts either to walk or to run; and those creatures are moved according as they receive their moving from that local motive power: but if a leg be defective, be out of joint, or crooked, that motion hath halting in that course joined therewith; but that halting, as it is a moving, cometh from the moving power of the soul; as it is faulty and lame, it dependeth of the faultiness of the leg which was broken. And thus it is as touching that continual moving, wherewith God stirreth his creatures. There is indeed a common influence, and it is received in things according to the quality of them: so the subject of deformity or privation is of God; and the moving of God sometime passeth through the mind corrupted, whereupon the fault of the action is not of God, but is drawn from the next cause. But what it is that God there doth, and how he governeth that deformity, is declared before: now we treat of the act which breaketh forth from our will. Wherefore it is rightly said, that the privation of righteousness followeth not the work of our will, and the motion thereof, so far forth as it is in the kind of nature, but as it is in the kind of moving.

Augustine in his seventh book De civitate Dei, the 30th chapter saith; that God doth so govern his creatures, as he permitteth them to exercise and work together with him their own proper motions. For God dealeth not alone, but (as I said before) the wicked men, and the devil also do use their naughty endeavor in working. But when we say, that the act itself (which afterward through our own fault is evil) is brought forth by the chiefest cause, that is by God; and by us, that is, by our will: how shall we understand this? Whether that God do it wholly, or we wholly? Or whether it be partly from him, and partly from us? And here we draw this producement to the very act of our will. We answer; If consideration of the whole be referred unto the cause, we must speak after one sort; if it be referred unto the effect, after another sort. If the whole be referred to the cause, so that we understand our will to be the whole cause of the action, that it be able by itself to work without God, it is not true: for unless God would assent thereunto, it should not be able to bring forth action. So God, although by his absolute power he might perform the work itself by himself, yet as the course of things is, he will not deal alone, but will have the creature to be a doer together with him: by this means are neither the will nor yet God, said to be the whole cause. But if it be referred to the effect it self, God and the will are the full cause; for God and the will make the whole effect, although they be joined together in action. I will show the thing by an example; For bringing forth of an action, we have a will and an understanding, and our will maketh the whole effect, and our understanding is the cause of the whole effect; but the one is nigh, the other further off. And so is it of the will and of God; the will doth all, and God doth all; but one is the first cause, and the other is the second.

22. As touching the third point, the sin which followeth is sometimes said to be a punishment of the sin that went before; and so God is said to punish sins with sins. Then if the sins, which follow, be weighed

as they be punishments, they after a sort be attributed unto God; not that God doth instill new naughtiness, or that he driveth men directly unto sinning; but when he hath withdrawn his gifts, then doth sin follow, whereby the mind is destroyed. And those destructions, and those wounds of minds, as they be punishments, they come unto us by just desert. Hereof we read in the first chapter to the Romans; that God gave them up unto a reprobate sense, as we have declared before. And that sin hath the respect of punishment, insomuch as it corrupteth nature, it is manifest. Augustine saith, and it is usually received; Thou hast commanded Lord, and truly so it is, that every sin is the punishment of him that sinneth. This also do the Ethnics acknowledge, Horace saith;

> The Sicill tyrants yet could never find,
> Than envy, greater torment of the mind.

Those evil affections do dry up the bones, made feeble the strength, and do afflict the minds; yet this is justly done: for God is just and righteous in all his ways. But if we be deprived of grace, we have deserved the same.

23. Wherefore we conclude this question of ours, and say; that, To speak properly and plainly, God is not the author of sin; neither would he sin to be. And yet is not God said to be the unperfecter, or the weaker; because he cannot make sin: for that is not imperfection and impotency, but perfection. These things cannot God do, because he is the chief good, and the chief perfection: nay rather, he establisheth laws against sins, he crieth out against them, and he punisheth them. And marvel not, when I said that God cannot properly will sin; for then might he turn away men from himself, then should he deny himself to be God. Paul saith unto Timothy; God cannot deny himself. By which reason Barnard

in his little book De praecepto and dispensatione was moved to say, that God can undo somewhat of the precepts in the second table, but not of the first table. Of the second he did relinquish something, as when he willeth Abraham to kill his son; so likewise while he commanded the children of Israel that they should carry away other men's goods: but whatsoever things be of the first table cannot he remitted. If God would not be loved and worshipped, he should deny his own self. If he be the chiefest good, should we not love and worship him? And some allege this reason; that The good things which belong unto our neighbors, be particular; and God can take away any private good thing, to put a greater in place. But those things which appertain to the worshipping of him, have respect to the universal good, and therefore cannot be taken away. Augustine in his book which is entitled Confutatio catholica quorundam sibi falso impositorum, the third chapter saith; Whatsoever is condemned in any man, is far from the author of nature. In the same place; That opinion is to be detested, which holdeth God to be the author of any naughty deed, or of any naughty will.

24. Now have we generally declared the proper causes of sin; but to show them particularly, we say that the cause of sin is man's will, his understanding, his depraved sense, his licentious appetite, the show of good which offereth itself (for nothing is desired of us, but in respect of some good.) Here withal the corruption remaining of original sin, from thence as out of a standing puddle, do always breath out evil affections. A cause also is our own infirmity and ignorance, also the suggestion of the devil and of naughty men; who nevertheless are able to prevail no further than God doth give them leave. There be ill examples also, sin itself is the cause of sin; for some prodigal men stealeth for the satisfying of his lust. Wherefore seeing there be so many true causes of sin, we must not make God to be author, to the intent we may excuse ourselves. Now it may

appear, that the wicked opinion of the Libertines must be condemned, who excuse all manner of sins. They which make God to be the cause of evil, but yet not so as we should be excused, seem not well to expound this question. In like manner is it of them, which allow but of a bare permission.

First therefore (to gather all into few words) we have said, that God is not properly the author of sin; secondly that God, when he will, doth justly withdraw from us his grace, which should be the hindrance of sin. Moreover, we have showed that God doth so govern sins by his providence, as they shall not rage any further than he permitteth; and in no otherwise than may be expedient for his providence. We have declared that God doth sometimes suggest both inwardly and outwardly, such things as in their own nature be good; but if they fall into corrupt men, they become occasions taken and not given of sins. Also that God doth not let, but permit sins; and that the same permission is not altogether without the will of God. Further, that seeing sin is a falling away and privation, it hath no need of an efficient, but of a deficient cause. Further, that our motion of turning away from God, is proper unto our will, as it is corrupted, not as it was instituted by God. We said also, that the guiltiness dependeth on God; and then, that the action which is the subject of deformity, cometh as well from God as from us, in the kind of the cause. And we showed, that sins are punished with sins. And last of all, we reckoned up the true causes of sins.

25. But now hereafter we will examine the former reasons alleged. They which denied God to be the cause of sin, as we also say, used these reasons. In the first, Augustine said in the 83rd book of questions, quest. 3. A man is not made the worse, by having a wise man to be author: neither is he therefore [the worse] by having God to be author. I grant it; for man became not the worse, in respect that God gave a

law; for by his law, he commanded not evil: neither is man become the worse, as touching the natural act which God bringeth forth; but he becometh the worse by reason of his backsliding, whereof we ourselves have deficient causes in our selves. Wherefore the devil, wicked men, our own sensuality, and especially the corruption of our own will do make us the worse. And so it is granted that we are not made the worse by God or by man. The second reason; Fulgentius saith, that God is no revenger of the things, whereof he himself is the author. We grant the argument; God doth not revenge that act, as it is a natural thing, as it dependeth of him; neither [doth he revenge] his own government which he useth, but the naughtiness which proceedeth from us, and which cometh from our own selves. The third reason; God hateth not those things which he maketh, but he hateth sin. The reason is firm. But the doubt is, that if he verily hate sin, why he doth not forbid it, seeing he may.

Scarcely can human reason discern God's perfect hatred against sin, seeing he taketh not the same quite away. Doubtless it is a difficult thing. Howbeit it cometh oftentimes to pass, that something which displeaseth, is, for some good end and purpose, not taken away; whereof there are plenty of examples in the state of man's life. There happeneth some man to be diseased in the body, whereby the corruption breaking out, there ariseth a grievous sore in some member; notwithstanding that this be very painful unto him, yet because he knoweth that it will turn to the benefit of his body, he suffereth the pain, neither doth he stop the sore. Also among the good corn there springeth up cockle and darnel; it displeaseth, yet are they not quite rid away, because men stand in fear, least the corn should be plucked up. So might we say of God, he hath his ends; namely, that not only his goodness, but also his righteousness may be declared: and therefore he hateth sins; yet not so, but that he will accomplish by them such an end as he hath prescribed.

Other arguments; If he did make sin, he should be a sinner; and if he would induce us to sin, he should do against his own nature: for natural things working, endeavor to make that which they do, like unto themselves. These arguments be firm. Neither is the action of God and working together of the creature, that is, of man's will, so to be affirmed, as if we ourselves apply not our own lewdness. God might seem to deal hypocritically, if he should on the one part command good things; and on the other part should will sin. I answer, that the argument would be of efficacy, if it might be said that God poureth in new lewdness: but in that he governeth sin, he worketh nothing against his law. Moreover, we must distinguish as touching the will of God, what respect it hath towards the commandments, and towards men. The commandments written we say are the will of God, for they express his nature and property: but if we mark how the will of God is towards men, and do say, that God would equally further all men to the keeping of his commandments, and that he giveth his grace equally unto all men, this must not so be allowed: for God hath his elect, and hath others also whom by his just judgment he overskippeth, and leaveth to sin and destruction. The Lord saith; I will have mercy upon whom I will have mercy: that is, Upon whomsoever it liketh me, I will have mercy. But they say that Men have free will, whereby they be able to keep the law of God, if they will themselves; and that there is no difference to be put in the help of God and grace, which is not given to all men after one sort. But I affirm that there is free will in God, he is free in his election, and in distributing of his graces: but his freedom dependeth not of us, who shall verily be free, if the son will make us free.

Wherefore in the law or commandments, God showeth what his property is, and what he judgeth to be right: but as touching the favor, wherewith he favoreth particular men, to keep those commandments, the question is otherwise. It was said, in the second of Chronicles; God rose up early, and sent his prophets unto them, wherefore he is no cause of sin. It is most true; God did so; but yet those suggestions, which in their own nature are good, fell into men, which were naughty of nature; who through their own lewdness were made the worse by those admonitions: for by their own fault they were stirred up to sin. God gave that warning, to the end he might spare his people; and the warnings were such, as being received, they brought pardon with them. But yet we must not say, that it was the determination of God to save them wholly at that time; for he upon just cause did withdraw his grace from them, and they of themselves, neither could nor would obey the admonitions of the prophets. The son of God wept for the destruction of Jerusalem: and this happened for sin; wherefore God will not that sins should be. I grant, that sins are not done properly by the will of God. Why then did he weep? He was now our neighbor, and the evils of his neighbors could not choose but make him sorrowful: also he knew that sin was against the will of God, although he were not ignorant that it could not be done without his will.

26. It is written in the prophet Hosea; Thy perdition cometh of thyself, O Israel, but thy salvation cometh of me. The sentence is most true: for seeing that sins proceed from ourselves, as from the proper causes, perdition also is of ourselves. The guiltiness or bond to abide the punishment, may be said to come from God: but that (as we said before) is not properly called sin, but belongeth unto righteousness. John the eight; The devil, when he speaketh a lie, speaketh of his own. It is most true; God instilleth not malice into him, but yet he is wont to use his falsehood, even as he doth other things. We read in Jeremiah; They ran, and I sent them not. In that place there is no speaking of the providence of God, but of the lewd dealing of false prophets, which feigned themselves to have received the word from God, their own conscience bearing

them record that God spake not unto them. They said, that they had dreamed dreams, and they vainly babbled that God had revealed some things unto them, when as nevertheless they lied, and knew that they did lie. Wherefore no reproaches ought to be laid against God for this matter, as though it should not be lawful unto him by his providence to use their lies.

This is the condemnation of them, that light came into the world; but men loved darkness more than light: wherefor God is not the cause, but they which loved darkness. We grant the argument; The will of man, of his own proper naughtiness, hath in it the motion of turning away from light to darkness. It was said; that God tempteth no man: but if he were the cause of sin, he should tempt men. As touching that place, understand it after this manner. It is not there spoken of every kind of temptation, otherwise the word should not be true. For God sometime tempteth his people, not that his own knowledge may be augmented, but that men may know him; and that others also may see how great things God hath wrought in them, and what grace he hath bestowed upon them. Also there is a certain kind of temptation to be desired: as in the psalm David saith; Tempt Lord or prove me, examine my reins and my heart. Neither must we forget that which we affirmed; namely, that God doth sometimes suggest inwardly and outwardly, things which in nature be good, and are received according to the disposition of men; neither must these kinds of temptations be removed from God. But James speaketh of inward lusting, whereby properly are suggested evil things, which provoke us to do against the law of God. Neither doth such lusting depend on God, except so far forth as he doth not resist it: even as also he doth not always hinder the devil.

It was added; that God might seem to deal tyrannically: whereto we answer, That he doth not properly stir up men unto sin; but yet he useth the sins of wicked men, and also guideth them, least they should pass beyond their bounds. It is added; How should he judge the world? For if he were author of sin, he should judge himself. We say that God shall justly judge the world: for what wickedness soever men do, they do it against the law of God, they do it willingly, and of their own accord, not by constraint: and The spirit of God shall reprove the world of judgment, of sin, &c. Besides this it was inferred, that by this means it would follow, that there be wills in God one repugnant to another. We answer, that in God, as concerning his nature, there is but one absolute and only will, which is the essence and nature of God: but yet, if we consider moreover the sundry objects, it may be called manifold. In respect of his commandments it is just, good, and one only: but in respect of men, some it promoteth, and other some it justly depriveth of God's favor. But they be no repugnant wills, because they be not occupied about one thing. Certainly such things as be repugnant, it behooveth that they be referred to the self-same subject. A father hath two sons; his will is, that the one should attend unto learning, and the other not. But be there two wills of the father? No forsooth; it is but one, and he doth rightly, so he do it upon good consideration.

Moreover James, in the fourth chapter saith; Ye say, We will go into such a city: ye ought rather to say; If God will, we will do this or that thing. Wherefore the will of God is, not only as touching the law and commandments; but it is also concerning those things, which be daily done of men. And that will belongeth not to the commandments: for these things are not contained in the Decalogue, and they after a sort be things indifferent. Very well did Augustine write in his Enchiridion unto Laurence, in the 102nd chapter; The omnipotent God, whether through his mercy he have pity upon whom he will; or through his judgment shall judge whom he will; doth nothing unjustly: neither doth he otherwise than with his will. Afterward it was said; If he should be a cause of sin, to what end tend so many warnings, and so many obtestations of his, by the son of God, by the prophets and apostles? We say, that these things are not done in vain; nay rather, they bring profit and utility. First they which admonish, rebuke, and exhort, do obey the commandments of God, who would this to be done. But thou wilt say; It will not profit me, the event must be committed unto God. Further, these things do profit the saints, which are predestinated; though it appear not presently, yet in some case they have their fruit: doubtless they make the ungodly the less excusable. Of this matter read in the book of Augustine De correctione and gratia; for these things were also objected to him.

27. It was argued, that If the matter should be on this wise, all difference between good and evil would be taken away; all things without exception should be the works of God, as the Libertines do say. We grant, that if God were verily the cause of sins, the Libertines should say rightly, but their opinion is detestable. The judgment of consciences would be taken away, inward accusations, and repentance would be dispatched, a window would be opened unto mischiefs, giving of thanks would be withdrawn; for we would delight in sin, and a great deal of the estimation of God would be lost. All these things be most true, but they make not against us; for we affirm not God to be truly the cause of sin. Lastly was brought forth, that God would have all men to be saved: if he will this, he useth good means, not evil; therefore he is not the cause of sin. We most plainly confess, that God is not properly the cause of sin: but yet out of this place I affirm with Augustine in his Enchiridion the 103rd chapter, that the sentence must not be so absolutely understood, as though there were not some, which God would not have to be saved. This sentence (saith he) is thus meant; God hath his elect among every state and condition of men; so in this respect, he accepteth not the person. He calleth

kings and private men, bond men and free men, man and woman. And excellently well doth this interpretation agree with the place of Paul. He had commanded to pray for princes: but some man might have thought, that the condition of them was such, as salvation should be repugnant therewith. In no wise (saith he,) God hath his elect among every kind of men.

The like reason he bringeth there, out of the 23rd chapter of Matthew; Ye tithe mint and rue, and every herb; that is, all kinds of herbs that are among you, not which be in India and Europe: for how could they tithe herbs of all the world? From which opinion disagreed not he that was author of the book De vocatione gentium, which they attribute unto Ambrose. For he saith, that God hath his generality; wherefore he judgeth that this general proposition must so be restrained, as if it were said, that God would have them to be saved, which belong unto his flock and number: even as, when it is said; All shall be taught of God: And again; All flesh shall see the salvation of God. Another way, whereby Augustine understandeth this place, is even there also; We understand (saith he) that none shall be saved, but such as God will have to be saved. As if thou shouldest say; A Grammarian is at the city of Tigurie, which teacheth grammar unto all: he saith not, all the citizens, but that there is none which is taught grammar, whom he teacheth not.

And so likewise he understandeth [that place,] He lighteneth every-one that cometh into this world; that is, How many soever be lightened, are lightened by this word. But that he would all men absolutely to be saved, he saith it is not true. For in the eleventh of Matthew it is written; Woe be to thee Chorazin, Woe be to thee Bethsaida: for if the miracles that were done in the city of Tyre and Sidon, had been done in you, they had long ago repented of their wickedness in sackcloth and ashes. Christ would not show forth the power of miracles among them, who (he said) would have repented, if they had been showed forth. And he addeth; Expound it which way ye will, so we be not compelled to believe that God omnipotent would have something to be done, and is not done: when as the truth speaketh, that All things, whatsoever he would have done in heaven and earth, he hath done: and surly what he would not, that hath he not done. And thus much touching the arguments made unto the 1st part.

28. Now let us take their arguments, which affirm God to be the cause of evil. In the first to the Romans it is said, that God gave them up to a reprobate sense. The interpretation is easy; he gave them up to the desires of their own heart, as afterward he himself expoundeth it: wherefore these desires were first evil. What did God? Verily he permitted them to obey their own naughty desires; he himself did not evil, but, in leaving them destitute of his grace, forthwith wicked desires took place in them; privation of itself followed: howbeit God used their naughty desires to the performance of his justice, namely, in punishing of them. Of the hardening of Pharaoh's heart, it is sufficiently declared before. In the sixth chapter of Isaiah, when God saith by the prophet; Blind thou the heart of this people, that they hearing may not hear, and seeing may not understand, &c. This is two ways to be expounded. Jerome for interpreting of these words, taketh a place out of the 11th chapter to the Romans, where it is said of the Ethnics and Hebrews; The Gentiles were in times past unbelievers, when ye did believe, but now they have obtained mercy, through your unbelief. While the Gentiles believed not, the Jews seemed to have the true worship: and on the other side, when preaching was afterward offered unto them, and they believed not, the apostles forsaking them, turned to the Gentiles: and so they were to become unbelievers, to the end that the Gentiles might be admitted unto grace. Thus did God use the incredulity of the Jews, and therefore he

added; that God did shut up all under unbelief, that he might have mercy upon all. Wherefore that same blinding of the unbelievers was, to do service to the providence of God, which the prophet foreshoweth.

Another interpretation there may be, and that more commodious. God's mind was, that Isaiah should be sent to preach; but least he might be discouraged afterward, when he should see their obstinacy, and that they were offended at the word, God telleth him before, that the same would come to pass. The word of God of itself hath not this, but he justly withdrew his spirit and grace from them. This word of thine (saith he) will be an occasion taken, through which they shall become more blind, and be turned away from me. This must be understood as touching the greater part; for there were some good men among them. Unto this end it is declared, that this should come to pass, that they by perishing, might make manifest the justice of God; who of his just judgment would make this their blindness to do him service. But that the blindness came of God, we must not understand it otherwise, then as touching outward things; for he offered them his word by Isaiah.

29. Another place; Lead us not into temptation. It is so spoken, as though God doth lead some into temptation, and by that means is the cause of sin. This sentence of the Lord Augustine in his book De natura and gratia, the 58th chapter interpreteth; To the intent we may resist the devil, we pray that the devil may fly from us, when we say; Lead us not into temptation. Therefore also are we warned, as it were by a grand captain exhorting soldiers, and saying; Watch and pray, least ye enter into temptation. Wherefore Augustine in that place referreth these things unto the temptation of the devil, who is able to bring nothing to pass further than God will give leave. And in the 67th chapter of the same book he addeth; Two manner of ways we provide against the diseases of the body; namely, that either they may not happen at all; or else if they

do come, that we may quickly be delivered of them. Thus when we say, Lead us not into temptation, we desire that God may turn away sin, that it happen not: but if we have fallen, and committed sin, we pray him that he will remit and forgive it. The same author against the two epistles of Pelagius, in the fourth book and ninth chapter, by the testimony of Cyprian writeth, when it is said; Lead us not into temptation, that we be warned of our infirmity and weakness. For it is said by the Lord; Watch and pray, least ye enter into temptation: the reason is added; For the spirit is ready, but the flesh is weak: let us not be insolently puffed up. In this place, temptation is ascribed to the flesh, and to weakness; so as God is excluded from being author.

In his book De bono perseverantiae, and sixth chapter, he saith, that Cyprian bringeth in that particle in these words; Suffer us not to be led into temptation: for he seeth that the devil can do no more than God hath given him leave to do. And God, as touching his own people, bringeth to pass, that he shall not prevail: but as touching the wicked, if he have the over hand, God cannot be blamed; unless he will say he is to be blamed, for that he hindered not, and that he ruleth evils, and useth them according to his providence. Here we objected, that it can hardly be, that the punishment and the fault should be all one. For it is called sin, in that it is voluntary; but punishment is always laid upon men against their wills. And how agreeth it, that voluntary and not voluntary should be all one? We answer, that we may consider our will as touching sin two manner of ways; one way, as sin proceedeth from thence, and is brought to effect by means of the same, and in that respect it is called a voluntary thing; another way, sin is considered as it is in the mind or will, and deformeth it, and after this sort it cannot be voluntary: for no evil men would have their mind to be polluted, wounded, or destroyed. Wherefore sin, as it is brought forth from the will, being the effectual cause, is voluntary; but as it bringeth in blemish or deformity, it is done against the will: for we would be all perfect. It was added; God is the cause of the cause of sin, therefore also the cause of sin. By what things do we sin? By the will and affections, the which God hath brought forth; therefore he is also the cause of the last effect. We answer, that sin dependeth not of the will and affections, as they were made by God; but as they are now corrupted: I showed an example before of halting.

30. Besides we said, that God removeth his grace and holy spirit, which do hinder sins, and therefore, &c. This we grant, but we add, that he doth justly remove his spirit. Indeed the removing of that which letteth is a cause; but yet that is not the proper cause: for there do also rest in us inward causes of evil. He giveth occasions; It is true, he suggesteth both outwardly and inwardly, but yet good things; the which, men through their own lewdness do use amiss. But he not only giveth occasions, but he also gave out his commandments. He said unto the devil; Go forth, do this: hereof will I note a few things. The prophet, by the figure Prosopopoeia, doth as it were bring in God to sit upon a seat like a judge: he would that Ahab should be slain, he seeketh who shall deceive him. Whereunto tendeth this inquisition? It putteth us in mind, that this should else-where be sought; because it is not in the nature of God, to deceive. The end is there set forth by his justice; he willeth that Ahab should now be slain. Divers ways are devised, this spirit showed one way, and that spirit another way: to the intent we may understand, that the providence of God hath innumerable ways, whereby he can punish men.

Those ways were there propounded, but not put in practice; because the providence of God was not minded to use them. A spirit stepped forth, who said; I will deceive him. Hereby it is gathered, that devils are prompt and ready to deceive; and when they do deceive, it is of their own doing. In the mean time we be taught, that those spirits be able to do no more than God doth give them leave: and in respect that he will use them, they be executioners [appointed] of God. Wherefore God said; Go forth: this is the imperative mood. If we respect the end, it was to slay and punish Ahab. But this leave was given, to the intent that the devil should exercise his naughty will, and deceive. And God used the sin of the devil, and would not hinder his work, nor yet let Ahab, but that he should believe the false prophets. Augustine, in his book of the 83. questions, quest 53. noted three things; The first is, that that which God did against Ahab, he did it by judgment; secondly, that he did it by an angel, and not by himself; thirdly, he saith not by every manner of angel, but by an evil angel; ready of his own nature to deceive.

It was said, that sin is a motion, and a certain action, and that the first mover is God: nothing is concluded, but that the subject of sin, that is, the act itself, hath will to be the nearest cause, and also God himself, in respect it is a natural thing. The saying of Augustine De gratia and libero arbitrio the 21st chapter, is expounded of the inclination unto good by himself, and unto evil indirectly. Also the dealing of Roboam, and the stirring up of the Philistines, and that Amazias would not hearken unto the warnings of the king of Israel's prophet, appertaineth to the justice of God: God was minded to punish them. As touching the words of Ahia the Silonite, for performing whereof, &c. These things were not done, because they were foretold; but foretold, because God foresaw that they should be. And to the end that they might so be, he appointed them for punishments of the wicked; and he knew how he would use them, and his reasons were allowed of God. It is written in the 14th chapter of Ezekiel; If the prophet be deceived, it is I that have seduced him. Here have we nothing else, but that the sin of the false prophet may be two ways considered. As it proceedeth from the will of an ill prophet, so it displeaseth God; and therefore he said he would punish it: but if afterward the use of it should be weighed, that God by such seducing would be revenged of the people, then he did justly withdraw his grace from them further, he used that seducement, which properly and by itself may not be ascribed to God.

31. There was brought a place out of the 21st chapter of the Proverbs, where it is said; that The heart of the king is in the hand of God, and he inclineth the same which way soever he will. The proposition is general; Which way soever he will, he inclineth the same. Here is no exception; therefore as well unto good things, as unto evil things. In the twelfth of Job, it is said; that God doth take away the hearts of them that be rulers of the earth, and that he maketh them stagger like drunken men. And how these things must be understood of inclination, I have declared. Wherefore I understand this sentence of Solomon no otherwise, than those words of saint Augustine, in his book De gratia and libero arbitrio; to wit, that he inclineth our wills unto good or evil, according to his good pleasure. Another argument was out of the 105th psalm, where it is said; God turned their heart, so as they hated them. What manner of turning that is, which he made in their harts, Augustine doth teach very well in the same place; it was no good heart that God made evil. But such is the goodness of God, that he useth both angels and men; and when they be evil, he piketh good things out of them. He increased the Israelites with children and with wealth; these things were good: wherefore God, by doing good unto the Hebrews, turned the heart of the Egyptians unto hatred; for hatred ariseth through other men's felicity. Wherefore God turned their heart, which naturally was evil, unto a hatred against the Hebrews; not by making of their heart evil. Ye see therefore that I feigned not, when I said that God suggesteth either inwardly or outwardly, such things as in their own nature be good; but through our fault do come occasions of sinning, but yet occasions taken, not given. And the occa-

sions which be offered, be not the furthest removed causes, as is the fir tree hewn upon mount Pelion; but they be immediate occasions, which stir up our desires: even as the Hebrews happiness was the immediate occasion, why the Egyptians envied them.

Isaiah the 63rd chapter; Wherefore hast thou made us to err, Lord? Which saying Jerome interpreteth of God's loving kindness. God did not straightway punish their sins; wherefore they began to contemn his judgments: God did suggest this his mercy in them, which was good; but through their fault, it was drawn to contempt. They may also be the words of the wicked, which cast upon God the cause of their sins. Or else the godly, when they think themselves, by the just judgment of God, to be forsaken of his grace; and afterward, they acknowledging their sins, speak after such a sort: doubtless not in blaming of God, but in marveling at his judgments. But howsoever thou understand it, God is exempted from the fault. It is written in the fourth of Jeremiah; Thou, O Lord, hast seduced thy people. Jerome answereth, saying; Those things, which were now spoken, seemed unto the prophet to be repugnant to the other words, which were spoken in the third chapter before: where God declared unto him, that Jerusalem should be called the seat of God, and that all the heathen should flock about it. But now God said, that The heart of the king, and of the princes should quail, the priests and people should be astonished: and therefore the prophet cried; Thou saidest, we shall have peace, but behold the sword. But the times (saith Jerome) must be distinguished; for those things, which were first spoken, were to be fulfilled after the captivity of Babylon: and that calamity, which was showed of afterward, was even at the doors.

32. Joshua saith, that God hardened the hearts of those nations of the Canaanites, that they should not make peace with Israel; because God was minded to cast them out before his people: and therefore he

seemeth to be the cause of sin. We answer with Augustine, out of the eight chapter, De gratia and praedestinatione: it is also entitled The book De voluntate Dei; What is it to harden? That he will not mollify: What is it to blinden? That he will not illuminate: what is it to enforce or reject? That he will not call. Which he speaketh, not of the general calling; but of that which is effectual; God poureth not in new hardness, which is not in the heart. Wherefore it may be said, that God hardened those nations; because he would not make them relent, whereby they might have made peace with the Hebrews: nevertheless, they were already to be destroyed, by reason of their own sins. But it is further objected, that no creature is appointed to perdition. God created not man, to the intent he would cast him off. And Jerome upon the prophet Abacuk, the second chapter is alleged; Although that the soul, by reason of the naughtiness thereof, be made a habitation for the Chaldeans; yet by nature it is the tabernacle of God. And no creature endued with reason is hereunto made, that it should be a habitation of the devil. Indeed these words doth Jerome speak. But if thou understand him absolutely, he is against the scripture, which speaketh otherwise. It saith, that The potter hath power of one lump, to make one vessel to honor, and another to dishonor. And it is said of Pharaoh; To this purpose have I raised thee, that I might show forth my power. God suffereth the vessels, prepared unto destruction, to the intent he may make his power manifest. It is also said by Solomon in the 16th of Proverbs; that The ungodly man is made for the day of wrath. In the epistle of Jude, there is mention of certain men, which were before ordained to this judgment, or to this condemnation.

But true it is, that this decree of God, before it be put in execution, hath just cause of condemning any man. For sins are committed in the meantime, for the which they that should be condemned, are condemned: yet is it the decree of God, that he calleth them not effectually; and surly that decree is just. But as touching Jerome himself, I answer; that the reasonable creature is not made, to the end he should be compelled to sin; for he sinneth through his own fault: yet it is in the decree of God, not to hinder that fault of his. I answer further with Zwingli, in his little book De providentia Dei, the sixth chapter; [Hereof] it would follow, that God doth procure theft, and such other things. He saith; proceed yet further, and thou mayest say, that this is done for the declaration of his justice. Then we see, to what end the reasonable creature is made; even that on the one side the goodness of God, and on the other side his severity may be declared. What wise man is there, that would ordain a thing to any such end, as he knew he could not attain unto? God fore-knoweth all things, he knoweth that the wicked shall be dammed; it shall not therefore be said, that he maketh those to salvation which shall be condemned.

Another argument was; If God would the end, he also would the means to come by that end. I grant; for he would that the patience of martyrs should be, therefore he would that persecutions should be. He would undoubtedly, but not after one manner; for that which is good, he would for itself sake: the persecutions which be done by tyrants, he would after a sort, that is, for some other consideration; he would suffer them, not hinder them; he would use those things. Where I say, that he would those things after a sort, it must not be inferred, that therefore he would them falsely, or like a subtle sophister. John saith; He that is borne of God doth not sin; that is to say, against the holy ghost, and without repentance. And seeing such a one doth some way sin, it must not be said, that he doth sin sophistically and falsely; for there is no such consequent: for he sinneth in very deed, and not sophistically and falsely. In like manner, the law of it self is holy; and yet after a sort, it is the cause of wrath and damnation: but yet not falsely nor sophistically; for so Paul himself speaketh, and that truly. Wherefore it followeth not, that God would after a sort, therefore he would that thing falsely and sophistically. But if God would those things, which be unto an end; and sins after a sort, because he hath determined not to let them, and is minded to use them: then his will being immutable, there shall follow an unavoidable necessity. I answer, that there shall be a necessity, but no constraint; and if our will be forsaken by the grace of God, it is in the necessity of sinning.

Verily, the providence of God, as touching his decrees, is as the iron and the adamant. For Zechariah as touching the chariots and empires, which should succeed after him; They went (saith he) through mountains of iron. The decrees of God are most steadfast. And Christ said; Those whom my father hath given me, none can pluck out of my hands. Yet there is somewhat, that may seem to withstand this saying. It is written in the 68th psalm; Let them be wiped out of the book of the living: wherefore if they be wiped out, who were written in before, the will seemeth not to be constant. Read Augustine upon that place; A man commonly saith, Quod scripsi scripsi; What I have written, that have I written: and will God wipe out that which he hath written? How then are they said to be wiped out? The kind of speech is according to the hope of them. In very deed, they were not registered, but they thought themselves to be registered. But there be some, which refer blindness and hardening of harts to foreknowledge only. Howbeit, there is not a bare prescience of these things, but there is a certain will of God, whereby God cannot foreknow things to come, unless they be such as shall come to pass. And those things that shall be, or be, cannot come to pass, or be, unless that God, with some kind of will, will have them to be, or to come to pass. Wherefore there is some will of God that precedeth fore-knowledge: he hath a will, not to let things; and he hath a will to use them according to his predestinated counsels.

33. Another argument; These tyrants Nebuchadnezzar, Sennacherib, and others, were in the hand of God, as a staff and rod; and therefore God seemeth to be the cause of sin. Indeed it is true that they were as a rod; and when they had executed their office, they were thrown into the fire: yet were they not without sense and perceiving, but were moved forward by their own naughty will, and therefore are justly punished. For there is two kinds of instruments, as I declared before. Howbeit this is no beguiling; that God will use these things, and yet command that they shall not be done. These men do them of a naughty will, but God useth their naughtiness. Men also can use well the naughty actions of their adversaries, and many times they do use them without any crafty dealing, even to the intent they may take heed to themselves, and may show patience. Sometime God useth sins, to punish the sinners themselves: yea rather, he useth them so always, for because sin is always a punishment of the sinner. And otherwhile he useth them for the punishment of others.

Another argument was; that God put into the heart of David to number the people. Indeed, the scripture speaketh after this manner. These kind of speeches we hear not in the poets, but in the word of God: Plato might banish poets out of his common weal, but we may not drive out scriptures, which speak on this wise. But how these things must be understood, I have declared before. God withdrew his help from David, he hindered him not; he would use that work for punishing of the people. But it is objected; If God withdraw his grace, he doth it justly. I grant it, yet notwithstanding he doth the same: further, he useth the devil also. In the book of Chronicles it is said, that the devil set on David; therefore God also did it, insomuch as he gave the devil leave. But they object against that, which we have oftentimes spoken; namely, that grace being removed from us, sin doth creep on of itself, seeing our own will, of itself inclineth unto it, even as darkness doth naturally come, after the light is gone. God (say they) is even as the sun, because his light shineth in every place; but there be men, which convey themselves into corners; but if his lightening be in every place, into what corners should men go where that light is not? The divine scripture saith otherwise: for it saith of him that abused the talent; Take it away from him, &c. David prayeth; Take not away thine holy spirit from me: wherefore God meant to use the sin of David for punishment of the people. And Aeschylus the tragical poet, is by some unjustly accused, who saith; that God, if he will destroy and take away any, he giveth the causes and occasions, seeing the scripture so speaketh, which can speak against the laws of Plato, but not against the laws of God. For it saith, that the sons of Helie did not hearken to their father, because the will of God was to destroy them: and that Roboam would not give ear unto the elders, because the turning away was of God.

It was said, that If the matter should be thus, then God should not be the cause of all things, if he be not the cause of sins. It followeth not; for although God be not the cause of sin, yet he governeth the sins, which be committed, he useth them, and maketh the very ground-work, so far forth as it is a natural thing. But it behooveth (say they) that sin be voluntary. If we speak of actual sins, it is true; but of original sin, it is not true. Also the first motions which be sins, are not voluntary. And Barnard in his treatise of free will, setteth down certain degrees of man's nature. Men that be blessed in the heavenly habitation cannot sin; it was in Adam, not to have sinned: after sin committed, we cannot choose but sin. So be the damned, so be the reprobate and wicked. But the godly and regenerate are able not to give place unto sin, and bring to pass that sin shall not altogether reign in them; and this they have of the spirit of God. Whereby it appeareth by this distinction, that the sin of the damned is of necessity; and yet sin nevertheless. For although it be a thing of necessity, yet it is voluntary; but not so voluntary, as we be able of ourselves to make choice of the other part, which is contrary thereunto: for we cannot have the choice on the other part, but through the same spirit of God. Sins are justly punished, but there is no respect had what thou art able or not able, but whether that which thou doest, be done against the law of God or no.

And God doth injury unto no man. Wherefore this objection is not of force, if we respect God. If one see a blind man to be falling, and doth not stretch forth his hand to help him, or setteth him not up again, it seemeth to be cruelty: God seeth a man ready to fall, he putteth not forth his hand, it seemeth to be cruelty. In whom? In men; because the law is prescribed unto them: God is not subject to these laws. This answer maketh Zwingli in his book De providentia, and in his book De falsa and vera religione, where he entreateth of merit. And although God bestow not so large gifts upon the reprobate, as he doth upon others; yet he giveth them many things. The preaching of the Gospel is set forth unto them, many other things giveth he unto all men, although he hath not mercy upon all unto salvation: God may do with his own what he will. These, thou sayest, reject his mercy. Jerome saith upon Jonah; God is merciful and pitiful of nature, ready to save those by his mercy, whom he cannot by his justice; but we cast away his mercy, which is offered. I grant it, insomuch as it is offered us by general preaching: nevertheless, God doth not change their wills; that he can do this, who denieth? If he will not, it is upon just cause that he will not. Augustine De bono perseverantiae, the fourth chapter, saith; that In one and the self-same thing, we see a difference of God's judgment; and in diverse things we see one judgment. There were two twins in the womb of Rebecca, before they had done either good or evil, yet is said; I have loved Jacob, and hated Esau. Some labored in the vineyard a whole day, others labored but one hour only, and yet received all one reward.

As for the instance of the goodman of the house, whose sons and servants do offend; I (saith he) enforce them not. The goodman of the house is rightly accused, because he hath a law: but God hath no law prescribed unto him, he himself hath prescribed to himself, that he will do nothing unjustly: but his will is the chief rule of justice. God forsaketh the reprobates, and is also forsaken by them, and he doth rightly. But in that he leaveth such as leave him, that is testified in the second book of Chronicles, the 15th chapter. The prophet Azarias, the son of Obed, saith unto king Amazias; Seeing that ye forsake him, he will forsake you. God is everywhere by his essence and his power, but in those that are his, by favor, grace, and ready help. He leaveth not the wicked in the two former sorts, but in the third. There was alleged the sentence of Anshelme De casu diaboli; If God (saith he) by a dishonest work, such as is adultery, do bring forth a child; why cannot that will of God, by a naughty will bring it forth as it is a natural thing? We grant that the subject may be brought forth of God; but afterward it behooveth to consider the defect in itself.

34. It is read in the acts, that they came together against Christ, to do whatsoever the hand and counsel of God had decreed; and that Christ was delivered by the determined counsel of God. Touching the death of Christ, the will of God hath another meaning towards Christ, then it hath towards the Jews. As touching Christ, God would that he should bear the cross, according to obedience and charity, because he is our redemption; and the divine nature brought to pass in him, that he did bear it. The Jews should deal so cruelly, God permitted them; but in that permission there was a will, not to hinder their naughty will, that he might use the same, and that redemption might follow. By this it appeareth, that he could have letted it, if he would; Could not my father (saith Jesus) give me eleven legions of angels to fight for me? He used that

sin to redeem us. Many good things were offered by God unto the Jews; such were the preachings, miracles, and reprehensions which he used, but through their default, they were taken in the worse part: wherefore they are left even in the necessity of sinning.

Where shall now be free will? It is lost. Augustine in the thirty chapter of his Enchiridion to Laurence saith, that After man had sinned, he lost himself, and his freewill also: he saith so twice in that chapter, and else-where also; and we have it in the second book of Sentences the 25th distinction. But Barnard saith, that it is not lost. These fathers disagree not if they be rightly understood; for Augustine taketh free will for free power of choosing things contrary, this or that. And while we be not regenerated, we cannot truly do acceptable things unto God, unless we be restored by the son of God; because free will, as touching those things doth not remain in us. Whereas Barnard saith, that free will remaineth, what is his meaning? He meaneth, that although men sin, they are not compelled, they have a consent, they are willing: and such free will remaineth. And he himself expounds himself, when he setteth down three sorts of liberty. He hath free will, from compulsion; from sin, when his will is regenerate; from misery, when he shall come into the kingdom of heaven. We have no freedom from misery in this life, from necessity we have; by necessity, he meaneth compulsion. This appeareth out of Barnard, for he placeth a freedom of will in God; he of necessity is good, and yet this taketh not away his free will. The angels, and holy men in the heavenly country cannot sin, yet they have a free will. Also he granteth a freedom unto the devil, and damned souls; and yet they cannot be good: but the evil which they will, they will it of their own accord, not that they be able to do the contrary.

The same author saith; It is grace which preserveth, and free will which is preserved. By what means? It taketh health willingly, that is, it assenteth, it consenteth: but he saith not that it consenteth of itself, nay rather he alledgeth the place of Paul; that We cannot of ourselves think a good thought, much less give our consent thereto: And; God worketh in us to will and to perform. God (saith he) without us, setteth before us good cogitations, by preventing us; afterward he changeth the will: he changeth (saith he) the affection, that the same being changed, the consent may follow. Wherefore he saith; that God doth four things in us; first, he stirreth up, by sending in good cogitations; secondly, he healeth, that is, he changeth the will; thirdly he confirmeth, that is, he leadeth to the act; fourthly, he preserveth, that we may not feel the want, that we may persevere, and that the good work may be accomplished.

35. To be brief, we also affirm that God, as concerning sin, is (as Epiphanius saith) <H&G>, that is, clear from the cause of all sin; because properly, he is not the cause, and yet he sleepeth not. This word also signifieth unblameable. God cannot be drawn into law by us; what he doth, he doth justly. And for our part we add, that it is a general opinion, and must still be retained in the church; that There is nothing done in the world, be it good or bad, without God's providence. Human actions cannot pass out of the bounds of God's providence, seeing All the hears of our head are numbered. If sparrows, being small silly birds, of the least estimation, do not light on the ground without the will of God; what shall we say of man's doings, the which so far excel? Divine providence hath an exceeding great scope; albeit it deal not all after a sort towards good things, and towards bad; yet are they not done without the providence of God, which is God's divine will, whereby things be mightily and very well governed, and directed to their own proper ends. Neither ought it to be any offense unto us, that he leaveth some evils in the world; for although they be against particular natures, yet they be available for common commodity. If all evils were taken away, we should

be destitute of many good things: wherefore it is said, that There would be no life of lions, if there were no slaughter of sheep, wherewith the lions be fed: neither would there be patience of martyrs, unless the cruelty of tyrants were permitted by God.

That which Plato writeth in the second book De Republica, seemeth to be against this doctrine of ours: he saith, that God is author but of few things unto men, because there be many evils amongst men, and God is the cause of none of them: whereby he seemeth to straighten the providence of God into a narrow room. If he mean the cause effectual, and speak of sins, we do grant it: and yet in the meantime providence is not in a profound sleep. But Plato in the same place hath, that, which must not be granted generally of the godly: for he denieth, that God cometh unto men in the likeness of strangers: but angels were entertained by Abraham and Lot in guest wise. Whereas he saith, that God cannot be changed, as touching his substance; it is true: but that he appeared sometimes in certain forms, it must be granted. He talked with Moses out of the burning bush; he declared himself upon mount Sina by voices; he exhibited himself unto the prophets by sundry likenesses. I think that Plato meaneth those vile changes, which the poets speak of; that he was changed into a swan, an eagle, or a bull: which things must in no wise be attributed unto God.

36. But whereas I said, that all things, whatsoever they be, are ruled by the providence of God; and that Platos saying can be no let, it seemeth not sufficient. For Damascene also is against it, who saith in his second book, the 29th chapter; that Those things, which be not in us, are subject to the providence of God: for he addeth, that the things within us are not of God's providence, but belong to our own free will. But shall not therefore our actions, which he saith are within us, be in the providence of God? Let them believe this that will; for I believe it not. He addeth

that which is more hard; namely, that The choice of doing things is in us, but that the perfection and accomplishment of good things is the work of God together with us. Who will say, it cometh from us, if we choose to be done such things as are good? The apostle saith, that God worketh in us, to will and perform. And whereas Damascene taketh away these things from divine providence, I like it not. He distinguisheth providence, into good pleasure and permission; these I am not against, I affirm both: namely, that providence not only ruleth good things, but that it also bringeth them to pass; and that it permitteth evil things, but yet not so as it permitteth them all wholly to themselves: for it useth them.

And he distinguisheth that same permission or good pleasure, and saith, that one is a dispensing and instructing permission; because it turneth to the discipline of saints, if they be left without help for a time. Sometime it is called a full grown permission, and as it were without hope of recovery; as when men, through their own default, perish and become past amendment. Even we also say, that God leaveth his elect for a time, but others forever. Moreover he saith; that God by an inward cause will have men to be partakers of salvation; but that he will afterward punish them when they offend. He calleth it a following will, as though it doth follow by our own default. I [for my part] say, that the will of God is of one sort, but that the objects be diverse. There is a chosen sort, whom he will have to be saved; and there be reprobates also, whom he will for their sins to be punished. But yet we must not there make a stay, he will show his power in them. Wherefore I affirm, that providence is universal, whatsoever Damascene saith. Of which mind Augustine also is in the 58th sentence, saying; that There is nothing done, either visibly or sensibly, which is not either commanded or permitted from the invisible or perpetual palace of the high Emperor: and so he excepteth nothing from the providence of God.

37. These be the things, that I thought meet to be spoken of concerning this matter. There remain many other things, but an end must be had. Indeed I know, that the reverend man Philip Melanchthon, whom I love and honor, seemeth to say otherwise: but here I appeal to the same man himself, in his old common places; read ye those things which be there, concerning predestination and free will. He saith, that the word [free will] which peradventure I would not have said, is most strange unto the divine scriptures, and from the judgment and meaning of the spirit. Further he saith, that Platos philosophy, in the beginning of the church, subverted piety. In the conclusion of that place; If we come (saith he) to our own inward and outward doings, those being referred to God providence, all things do come to pass even as they be appointed. But in outward actions, if they be referred unto will, there is a freedom [in us.] If we shall consider the inward good things, which God doth require, there he saith is no freedom: if our inward affects begin to pass measure, they cannot be staid. The same thing saith Ambrose upon Luke, and it is often alleged by Augustine, that Our heart is not in our own power. There be others also, which disagree not from them; of which number are Zwingli and Luther, the noble instruments of reformed religion; likewise Oecolampadius, Bucer, and Calvin: and I might allege others, but I strive not to bring many witnesses. I said, that to speak properly, God is not the cause of sin: and that there is nothing done in the world, be it good or evil, without the providence of God. But and if I have not hit the mark I shot at; I am sorry for it. If any man shall by any sufficient proofs show this opinion to be ungodly, or hurtful to good conversation, I am ready to alter the same. I have discoursed the more at large hereof, because it is a thing of great importance: and it falleth out oftentimes

in the holy scriptures. And things are better understood, which be set down to the full; than such as are declared here and there by piecemeal.

We have added these few things out of the like place upon the first of Samuel, the second chapter.

38. Now there resteth, that we speak of the very will itself of God. First of all I grant, that the distinction, which the schoolmen use to make, misliketh me not, when as they affirm, that the will signified is one, and the will effectual, or (as others write) the well pleasing will is another. The will signified is that, which showeth what we ought to do, or what we ought to avoid; for thereby we gather the judgment and ordinance of God, and that consisteth in the law, in the commandments, promises, threatening's and counsels: moreover to this kind of will belongeth that saying; Thou art the God that wouldest not iniquity: and that saying also; Thou hast hated lying and iniquity: and all those testimonies; by which it can be showed, that God would not have sins. And how I pray you can God be willing that sins should be, seeing he hath made a law against them; seeing he most severely punisheth them; seeing he hath planted in the minds of godly men the abhorring of sins; seeing for the taking away of sin he suffered his own well-beloved son to be put to death upon the cross? But we must note, that against this will of God, which is called the will of the sign, many things be committed and done. The number is great of wicked men, which contend against the law of God, which disquiet preachers, which slay the prophets; yea which in times past killed the son of God himself. Neither must we omit, that this is truly so named, and indeed the will of God, seeing Christ saith; He that doth the will of my father, the same is my mother, my brother and my sister. And it is written in Deuteronomy; What other thing will God, but that thou love him, and walk in his ways?

Moreover, the other will of God is that, which is called mighty, effectual, and according to his good pleasure, which by no power can be vanquished and overcome; seeing it is written thereof, that Whatsoever he would, that hath he done. Of this will Paul saith; Who is able to resist his will? And surly, if there might be anything done against God's will and mind, it would be weak and feeble. These two wills are so distinct, not as if they were two things and faculties which be placed in God; seeing that act appeareth to be most absolute. But forsomuch as God doth not always reveal his general and whole counsel unto men (for that is not needful, seeing it hath been enough for him to show that which is sufficient for obtaining of salvation) thereof it coms, that these two wills do differ. For what he hath by any means declared, that must be referred to his signified will; and whatsoever he hath kept to himself, as secret and hidden, that appertaineth to his well pleasing will. But to the end that this may be the easilier understood, it is meet to be showed by plain and notable examples. God commanded Abraham, that he should go to sacrifice his only son Isaac; certainly in this precept was contained his signified will: for God showed Abraham, that he would only make a trial of his obedience; and showed him not, that he would afterward let the sacrificing of Isaac; which prohibition doubtless did follow afterward; neither was his well pleasing will made manifest before. Wherefore we may decree, that his well pleasing will, and his signified will is all one; but is in sundry wise called, according as it is known or unknown unto us.

Besides this, it was said unto Hezekiah; Set thine house in order, seeing thou shalt now die. Certainly, there was no other way in the king but death, considering the force of his disease, and course of nature; and his death was the will of God, as it might be perceived both by a natural sign, and by the words of the prophet. Yet, because God, of his mercy, had decreed, upon his repentance and tears, to prolong life for many years;

this will of his was as well effectual as well pleasing. Also by his signified will destruction after forty days was denounced unto the Ninevites, when as nevertheless God, by his well pleasing will, minded to forgive them being penitent. This will is joined with the other; for they which fall from the one, do light upon the other: and they which reject that will of God, whereby he publisheth his law, his promises, his threatening's and counsels, do run into that, whereby sinners suffer punishment for their wicked offenses.

39. Wherefore Augustine in his Enchiridion unto Laurence, the 101st chapter, very well saith; That which God will have done, is in any wise done, either of us, or upon us: of us, when we live well; upon us, when we receive punishment for sins committed. And in the 102nd chapter he saith, that Sinners do as much as in them lieth against the law of God; but as touching his omnipotency they cannot. Yea, and Gregory wrote in his morals, the 11th chapter, and sixth book; Many do the will of God, when they endeavor to change the same: and in resisting, they unwittingly obey the counsel of God. Also Joseph answereth his brethren with this saying; You sold me indeed, but God's purpose was to send me before you into Egypt, that I might prepare for you both food and safety. Moreover, this is the same will, whereby God doth predestinate his elect unto eternal life; the which, as it is unknown unto us, so the same being most mighty, cannot be weakened. By this distinction of God's will, we understand sufficiently what answer we ought to make, when it is objected unto us, that God made man a living soul, and therefore would not that he should perish. For we say, that this is true as touching his signified will; for he offered unto man a law, promises, threatening's, and counsels: which things, if he had embraced, he had surly lived. But if we have respect unto that other mighty and effectual will, doubtless we cannot deny, but he would have men to perish. For as we read in the 16th of

Proverbs; God made all things for his own self, even the ungodly to an evil day. And Paul teacheth us, that God is like unto a potter, and that he maketh some vessels to honor, and some to dishonor. And this is also the same will, whereby God ruleth, governeth, and moderateth the naughty desires and sins of men at his own pleasure, as it hath been said before. By this will, God delivereth the wicked into a reprobate sense, sendeth in the Chaldeans to lead away his people into captivity, addeth efficacy unto illusions, would have the wicked to be seduced, and is said to harden them.

40. But seeing these things are expressly read, and that we oftentimes light upon them in the holy scriptures, we must diligently consider, how they should be understood. The common sort think, that whereas it is written, that God doth blind, doth harden, doth deliver, doth send in, doth be guile; nothing else is meant thereby, but that he suffereth these things to be done. After the which manner, very many of the fathers do interpret those speeches, being led doubtless by this reason; that they thought it a wicked and blasphemous thing, if God should be accounted the author of sin; and they would not that men should cast upon God himself the causes of their sins. Which counsel of theirs, I very well allow, and confess (together with them) that these things be done by the permission of God: for seeing he can inhibit sins to be done, and yet doth not let them, he is rightly said to permit or suffer them. Wherefore Augustine very well saith, in his Enchiridion unto Laurence, the 98th chapter, that There is no mind so wicked, but that God can amend the same, if he will: but not to prohibit, when thou canst, is to permit. And the same author against Julian, in the fifth book, the ninth chapter showeth, that There be many evils, which God would not permit, unless he were willing thereunto.

But there must be somewhat else also brought besides permission, if we will duly satisfy those places of the scripture, which are objected. For they which say, that God doth only permit, they cannot altogether exclude his will; because he permitteth the same either willingly or else unwillingly: unwillingly I am assured he doth not, because none may compel him; it followeth therefore, that he doth willingly permit those things to be done. Neither must we imagine, the same will of permission to be stack in God; for in God there is nothing that is not perfect and absolute. Wherefore it must of necessity be determined, that God doth not only permit sin, but also after a sort willeth it; yet not in respect that it is sin, (for his will is always of necessity carried unto good) but in that it is a punishment of wickedness done before: for in that respect, although it be sin, yet it goeth under the form of good. So do princes and magistrates other whiles set lions and wild beasts upon ill men, and encourage elephants against enemies; yet they made not those kind of beasts, but they cause the fierceness and cruelty of them to serve their use. So God useth the labor of tyrants, when he will take just punishment of any people.

Wherefore the king of Babylon is called the hammer, staff, and saw of the Lord's hand, when God would by his violence, chastise the people of Israel. For that king, notwithstanding he was the mightiest prince, was not able of his own force to afflict the children of Israel: nay rather, he was rebuked of arrogancy, because he sometime ascribed that thing to his own strength: for God declareth, that he himself was the very author of so great destruction. And Job, when he was so grievously vexed by the Sabees, by the Chaldeans, and also by the devil, and deprived in a manner of all his goods, he no less godly than wisely said; The Lord gave, and the Lord hath taken away. And that he might the more evidently show, that this happened by the will of God, he added; Even as it pleased the Lord, so it is come to pass: for he saw that God used the Sabees, Chaldeans, and the devil as instruments. And in the second book of Samuel, the 24th chapter, it is said, that God stirred up David to number the people: which act in Paralipomenon is attributed to the devil. Both with sayings be true, because God, by the ministry and work of the devil provoked him to do it. For even as Solomon saith; The heart of the king is in the hand of God, he inclineth the same which way soever he will: certainly, not by instilling of new evil, as we have oftentimes said before; but by using of the same which he hath [already] found, either to the punishment of sins, or else to the performance of his other counsels. Therefore, when it is written, that God doth either harden or make blind, we must believe that he not only forsaketh and leaveth; but that he also applieth his will.

41. Neither must we pass it over, that in the seventh and eight of Exodus, it is written, that God hardened the heart of Pharaoh, when nevertheless in the eight chapter it is written, that Pharaoh himself hardened his own heart, either of which is certainly true. For first Pharaoh had in himself the originals of so great an obstinacy, and he willingly, and of his own accord set himself against the word of God. But on the other part (as I have declared before) God provided, that the same his obstinacy should be openly showed, and did moderate and govern it according to his own pleasure. We must not think, that God doth so rule the world, as he should sit like an idle man in a watch tower, and there do nothing: or that he suffereth the world and inferior things, to have scope to wander at will, as doth a horse which hath the rains at liberty. Neither is that true, which is alleged by some, that God neither willeth nor nilleth those evils or sins; as if he thought not upon them at all. Even as if one should ask me, whether I would the French king should hunt this day or no, I might rightly answer, that neither I would it, nor would it not, seeing

the matter pertaineth nothing unto me. But as touching God, it cannot rightly be answered so; seeing what things soever are in all the world, they do belong to his care and providence.

But I would that these men did weigh with themselves, by what testimony of the scripture they be able to confirm that permission of theirs, which they so obstinately retain. I am not ignorant, that they allege for themselves, that which is said in the 81st psalm; I permitted them to their own hearts lust. But if we confer with the true Hebrew text, it will appear more feeble, and of less proof than they be aware of. For the verb Schillach in the Hebrew, is in the conjugation Piel, which by the force of the conjugation signifieth, A vehement action; neither is it convenient, that we should abate the force thereof, through expounding of it by the word Permission. Nay rather, it agrees with the phrase of Paul, wherein it is said in the epistle to the Romans, that God delivered the wicked to a reprobate sense: and it is rather showed, that God cast away the wicked, than permitted them. But whereto did he permit them, or cast them off? Verily to their own wicked desires; as who saith, they should be wholly possessed and governed by them. And in this sense is that Hebrew word oftentimes used in the scriptures. In Genesis it is showed, that God cast man out of Paradise; and who would there interpret the word Cast out [by the word] Permitted, seeing he rather drove and thrust them out from thence? Moreover, in the 19th chapter the angels say, And the Lord hath sent us out to destroy Sodom: in which place, To send forth cannot be the self-same that is to Permit. And it is written in Ezekiel; It brought forth the branch: while notwithstanding a vine doth not permit the branch to come forth of it, but doth rather enforce it to bud out. Wherefore let the interpreter beware, least in that place he interpret the Hebrew verb Schillach, by the verb of permitting.

42. Neither must we pass it over, that the holy scriptures no less attribute the permission of God unto good things than unto evil. For the apostle in the sixth chapter to the Hebrews, when he entreated of good things, saith; If God shall permit. Julian the Pelagian (as appeareth out of Augustine, in the third chapter of the fifth book which he wrote against him) was of the opinion, that when it is said in the scriptures, that God delivereth or blindeth; it must only be understood, that he leaveth or permitteth. But contrariwise, Augustine saith, that God doth not only permit, but (as the apostle taught) He declareth his wrath and power. Furthermore, Julian writeth, that such speeches are hyperbolical or excessive speeches: but Augustine affirmeth that they be proper. Julian interpreteth, that these which are said to be delivered to their own lusts, were infected before with these diseases: wherefor, he addeth; What need was it, that they should be delivered to them? It was enough that they were suffered to wallow and rest in them. Unto this Augustine saith; Doest thou think it all one, to have desires, and to be given over unto them? For the ungodly be given over unto their naughty lusts, not only that they may have them, but that they may be altogether had and possessed of them. Wherefore the same father added; Even as God dealeth in the bodies of wicked men, by vexing and punishing them; even so he worketh in the minds of them, by driving of them unto sins. And in the same place he entreateth of the history of Semei, where David saith; The Lord commanded him to curse me. The Lord (saith Augustine) justly inclined the will of Semei (being evil through his own fault) to rail upon David: and the cause is showed; For the Lord shall reward me good for this rebuke.

The same Augustine also in his book De gratia and libero arbitrio writeth, that God doth work in men's minds, inclining them as well unto good as unto evil, oftentimes by his secret judgment, yet sometimes by his manifest judgment, but evermore by his just judgment. Whereunto add, that how and for what cause he doth these things, it is exceeding hard to express. But yet this is most certainly to be determined, that these evils, so far forth as they come of God, be not sins; but are things just and good: but in that they proceed either from the devil, or from men; of good right they ought to be accounted sins. The Manichees, when they could not unwrap themselves out of this doubt, did feign, that there were two beginnings of things, whereof the one should be good, but the other evil. But we teach, that there is one God, the author of all good things; we say, that sins sprang up by the departing of Adam from God, and yet that those sins are tempered and ruled by the will and pleasure of God. Whereupon we conclude, that the very actions themselves, that is, the subjects of sins; be of God; and that he, when he thinketh it meet, doth withdraw his grace and succor, and that afterward he ruleth and bendeth the naughty lusts of men, which way soever it shall please him: and that seeing he useth the sins of men to the punishment of other sins, it cannot be said, that he by no means at all would them.

But of the sin of Adam the question is the more difficult, because there was no fall of his went before, which should be punished by God with a latter sin. Yet unto this we answer, that the action of his, that is, the subject of deformity and unrighteousness was of God; but the privation or defect came of the free will of Adam, whom God created uncorrupt, free and perfect; but yet not so, that he might not revolt and do amiss. Neither was the grace of God, whereby he should be kept back from falling, so great, as it did firmly establish him. And it cannot be doubted, but that God would that Adam should fall; otherwise he had not fallen: and he would have him fall, doubtless not in respect of sin; but that he might use that fall to make manifest his power, and the immeasurable riches of his goodness: and that he might show himself able, not only to make man pure and perfect; but to restore him also, being fallen and perished. And for that cause he sent his son to die for mankind upon the cross. Wherefore Gregory cried out; O happy fault, which deserved to have such a redeemer!

43. But this must be diligently marked, that God doth sometimes allow those things, whereas yet it pleaseth him not that they should be done. Not as though there be two wills in him; for he hath but one will only, whereof notwithstanding there be diverse objects: for he considereth our mind and determination, the which oftentimes he alloweth. But on the other part, he hath before his eyes, the order of his providence, the which by all means he willeth to be sound and steadfast. Therefore, he sometimes inspireth in our hearts, things which in their own nature should be good; yet for all that he will not have those things to be brought to an end, because they serve not to the order of his providence. So we say, that the prayer of Christ, wherein he desired to escape death, pleased God, although he would not fulfill the same. Neither did Christ, with a lewd or corrupt will, but with a righteous and good will, will that which he desired. But the providence and predestination of God remained immoveable, whereby he had decreed, that at the very same time he should be fastened upon the cross for our salvation. Wherefore we must religiously and godly meditate many things; but when we understand that God will not have those things to be done, our cogitations must be applied to his will. But to entreat of this thing with more perspicuity and plainness, let us first of all determine, that man's will ought after some sort to be made conformable to the will of God; for otherwise it should not be right: for that which is right must agree with the rule of God. Yet is it not of necessity, that what God would have to be done, should please us all manner of ways; because it is requisite sometimes, that the same

should displease us, and that rightly, and without sin. Which thing the better to understand, it shall be showed by examples.

Moses heard, that God would root out his people; he otherwise would, and sorrowed exceedingly: and that it might not be, he resisted it by prayer. Also Samuel knew that Saul was rejected, yet he did not forthwith settle his mind upon that will of God; but he heavily took the fall of that king, and for that cause he wept along time. And Jeremiah understood that Jerusalem should be destroyed, and he lamentably bewailed the ruin thereof. Here some say, that the decree or pleasure of God, is either known to us, or else unknown. When it shall be manifest unto us, we ought to bend our will unto him; but if it be hidden from us, we have a law revealed, which we may safely follow. Indeed these men say somewhat, but yet this saying of theirs doth not fully satisfy. For Jeremiah and Christ knew very well, that by the decree and will of God Jerusalem should be utterly destroyed; yet nevertheless they wept for the cause, and in weeping they sinned not. Moreover, it cometh oftentimes to pass, that even by the very works of God we know his will; wherein yet, we must not straightway repose ourselves: for sometimes it happeneth, that the son seeth the father die, which son if he be godly, he understandeth withal, that God's will is, that he should die. Shall he not therefore be sorrowful, and desire that his life may still be prolonged? What shall then be done, when such things do happen? Verily we must consider what is meet for the will of God, and what is convenient for our will.

Truly it agreeth with the will of God, that he should work according to his goodness and righteousness, to the end he may benefit the good, and punish the wicked: and it is fit for our will, that it should do those things which be agreeable thereunto. Also, what things are agreeable to our nature, we shall perceive by the constitution thereof; that is, by the law of nature and of God; and otherwhile also by an inward inspiration of the spirit: and thus, albeit we do in very deed disagree from the will of God, yet as touching the form and efficient cause, we agree with the same. For as much as God sometime, willeth two things at once, namely to punish a city, a nation, and our parents; and also that we for that cause should mourn: neither are these things repugnant one with another. In times past God willed Sodom and Gomorrah to be destroyed, which thing he declaring unto Abraham, Abraham was many ways sorrowful, and he entreated for them which should be destroyed; neither are we to think that Abraham poured out his prayers without the spiritual inspiration of God.

44. Furthermore, to these things this also must be added; namely, that the things which we know that God would, may be two ways considered. First simply and absolutely; in which respect we must do those things, which be agreeable to our will or nature rightly instituted: or else we must behold them, with a just comparison unto the divine providence, whereunto if we confer them, they must wholly rest thereupon; because (as Augustine in his Enchiridion saith) that It is a wicked thing to strive against the providence of God. Briefly it is our part in all things, to will that which God would we should will, and that to a right end; that is, with a good purpose: or (as men commonly speak) with a right intent; although as touching the matter, it behooveth not that that should always like us, which seemeth meet unto God. But if thou demand what those things be, which agree with our nature well instituted? I answer, things holy, honest and just. Wherefore the apostle said to the Philippians; Whatsoever things be true, honest, just, pure, profitable, of good report; if there be any virtue, or if there be any praise, those things think upon and do. And therefore David, when he determined to build the temple, although God would not have it done; yet was David's will allowed as

just and right. Our of doubt, the good king knew that God was willing to have a temple built into him, and he understood that it should be done at Jerusalem; wherefore his will dissented not from godliness. Moreover, seeing he was a child of God, and was stirred up by his spirit, no doubt, but God inspired him with that will.

Neither must we mark what God doth outwardly, but consider what he doth within us, and then we must follow that. He worketh in us both to will and perform; indeed not always a perfection of the work, or a will that is perfect and sound: neither are these two always so joined together, as he worketh at once both to will and to perform. For sometime he only worketh to will, and granteth not, that the thing which we will, shall come to effect. And not only our will ought to be conformable to the will of God, but also our understanding: for we ought to understand those things only, which God would reveal unto us, and no further. No man therefore hath said; I will understand those things which God himself knoweth. These things are largely entreated of in the first book of sentences, the 48th distinction; and in Augustine's Enchiridion.

Another discourse of the same argument.

I affirm the cause of man's sin to be the will or the free will of our first parents, who fell of their own accord, and obeyed rather the suggestion of the devil than the commandment of God; from whom afterward was derived original sin unto all the posterity: whereupon we have vice and corruption enough in our own selves. Wherefore God instilleth not in us a new naughtiness unto sinning, neither doth he bring in corruption; and therefore I do affirm our wills to be the causes of sin, and not God.

But the scripture saith in the epistle to the Romans, that God delivered up the Ethnics unto a reprobate mind, and unto vile affections. And in the second of Samuel it is said, that God stirred up David to number the people. And in the same history David said, that God commanded

Semei to curse David. In the same book the twelfth chapter, God said unto David by the prophet; I will take thy wives, and give them to thy neighbor, and he shall sleep with them: for thou didst it secretly, but I will do this thing before all Israel, and in the open sun light. It is said by others, that these speeches must be referred unto the permission; which thing I do not absolutely deny: for God, if he would, might have let these mischiefs, but he would not hinder them. Howbeit I add, that such a permission must not be granted, whereby some may affirm, that God dealeth so idly, and so leaveth the government of things, as he doth nothing about sins themselves.

[1] First, he taketh his gifts and his grace from certain men, because they abused the same; which grace being removed, and that justly, for a punishment of their former sins, men being destitute of that help, do fall into more grievous crimes. And that God doth sometime withdraw his grace, David knew well enough, when he sometime said; Turn not thy face from me, nor take away thine holy spirit from me.

[2] Secondly, God doth punish sins with sins; as it appeareth in the epistle to the Romans, and in the places now alleged. And sins, so far forth as they be punishments, do belong unto justice, and in that respect are good. Wherefore it is not unfit for God, thus by sins to punish former sins.

[3] Thirdly, he ruleth and governeth sins themselves; for he suffereth them not to rage so far out of measure, as the evil will of man desireth: he restraineth them, he keepeth them back, neither doth he suffer them to rage against every man, and at all times: also, he directeth them to the performance of his counsels; namely, to the trial of just men, and to the scourge of the wicked, and such like purposes. Wherefore the scripture saith, that fierce and cruel tyrants are in the hand of God, as staves, hammers, and saws.

[4] Fourthly, God sendeth in other occasions, which if they should light upon good men, they would provoke them unto good things: but because they light upon evil men, they are by those men's fault, soon taken in evil part, and are made occasions of sin. So Paul saith, that By the law sin was increased. And the words of God, spoken unto Pharaoh by Moses, were an occasion to express out of him blasphemies and hardness of his heart. Which thing God saw would come to pass, yet did he not restrain his own word, when he knew that Pharaoh would become the worse thereby; who nevertheless had the naughtiness in his own self, and took not the same of God.

[5] Fifthly, since that the defect of sin is only in human actions, the which are deprived of right government; the very action of man cannot be sustained, preserved, and stirred up, without the common influence of God, by which all things are governed and preserved: for truly is it said; In God we be, we live, and are moved. Therefore the defect, which properly is sin, proceedeth not of God: but the action, which is a natural thing, wherein the defect sticketh, cannot be drawn forth, but by the common influence of God.

These be the things, which I said that God doth by his providence and government about sins; although he be not the true and proper cause of sins. By which interpretation we may rightly understand, what those speeches of the holy scriptures, and sayings of the fathers do mean, wherein God seems to be made the cause or author of sin.

Chapter Five

How it May be Said That God Does Repent, and Does Tempt .

The interpreters labor earnestly to understand how repentance may happen unto God. For God saith; I am God, and am not changed. And in the first of Samuel; The triumpher of Israel is not changed. And Balaam in the book of Numbers saith; God is not as a man, that he should be changed: neither as the son of man that he should be a liar. Yet in Genesis he saith; It repenteth me that I have made man. Forsomuch as these places seem to be repugnant, they must be accorded together. Some after this sort expound these places, that Even as the holy Ghost is said To call and make request for us, with sighs that cannot be expressed; so it may be said, that God doth repent. But the spirit prayeth not, requesteth not, sigheth not; for he is God: but because he stirreth us to pray, to make request, and to sigh, he himself is said to do the same. And according to this sense Paul biddeth us, that we should not make sorrowful the spirit of God: that is to say, we should not with our wicked acts offend the saints, in whom is the spirit of God. Even so, because the wickedness of Saul was a grief unto good men, and that God stirred up that affection in them; therefore God himself is said to be led with repentance. This reason Luther followeth in his treatise upon Genesis. But Augustine in his book of 83 questions, the 52nd question, where of set purpose he handleth this question, saith, that The scripture is accustomed oftentimes to humble itself to our capacity, and to attribute those things unto God, which we see done in the life and conversation of men; for that the same cannot otherwise be understood.

Therefore, because men use not to revenge, unless they be angry; the scriptures say, that God, when he doth revenge, is angry. And because that men possess not the chastity of their wives, without jealousy; and that God in like manner taketh principal care, least his church being as it were his spouse should play the harlot, they say he is jealous. On this wise are feet, hands and other parts of the body ascribed unto God. And so, because men are not accustomed to change their purpose, unless they repent them of some deed; therefore, as often as God changeth his doing, they say that he is moved by repentance: not that there is become any alteration in God, but because that thing may be changed, which we hoped would have continued forever. And for this purpose it is said, that God repented him that he made Saul king. Others think that this doubt may more easily and plainly be dissolved, if the change be understood in the thing itself, and not in God. And to hold us to our example, Saul was godly and honest before, now he became wicked and rebellious; therefore he seemed worthily such a one, of whom God would repent.

And this seemeth the more probable, because it followeth in the text itself; And Saul went his way.

Look the propositions out of the sixth, seventh, and eight chapter of Gen.

2. The first opinion, although it may have some show, yet it cannot be allowed in every respect. Indeed it may be said, that God doth that which he bringeth to pass in us; and also causeth us to do it, but yet this holdeth not always. For he burned Sodom, he destroyed Pharaoh, and by that means exercised his wrath and revenge; yet he did not drive men to do these things. And we read that God repented him, and yet it is not written that Samuel repented him. Augustine's judgment is both plain and probable. The second opinion also may not be forsaken, wherein nevertheless it must be considered, that the change is said to be in the thing itself, and not in God. Jeremiah saith; If they shall repent them of their ways, I also will repent me of all the evil that I have threatened them. Therefore unto this changing in man, there followeth also a change of God's sentence; whether the same appertain unto the promise, or unto the change. For so often as a sinner doth repent him with a true faith, he is by and by delivered from everlasting destruction. But the sentence of temporal punishments is not always changed, although he repent him never so much. David was penitent for his adultery, yet the judgment of God, which Nathan pronounced, remained stable. Moses repented, and yet he might not enter into the land of promise. True therefore is this saying, as concerning the judgment of everlasting death; but not always touching temporal punishments.

Moreover, that change cometh not of ourselves, but of God: for so Paul writeth unto Timothy; If God peradventure shall give them repentance. And unto the Philippians; It is he that worketh in us to will and perform. We cannot once think a good thought, of ourselves, as of our selves. And unto the Corinthians the 15th chapter; I have labored more than all, and yet not I, but the grace of God that is in me. But it is in us (they say) to consent. Nay rather, the assent itself is also of God; for we have a stony heart, and unless the same be changed and made fleshy, nothing is brought to pass. And although they think it a small matter, while they say there is a consent of ours; yet if the same be attributed unto us, we shall have whereof to glory: for Who hath severed thee (saith Paul?) what hast thou which thou hast not received? And if thou have received, why doest thou boast, as though thou hadst not received? And; It is neither of him that willeth, nor of him that runneth, but of God that hath mercy. Here Augustine saith; If anything be left unto us, Paul concludeth nothing: for the proposition might be so turned, as it should be read on this wise; It is not of God to have mercy; but of man, that willeth and runneth. I know (saith Paul) there dwelleth not in me, that is, in my flesh, any good thing. And Christ saith; You have not chosen me, but I have chosen you. David also saith; Incline my heart unto they testimonies. And; A clean heart create within me, O God. But no man can create himself. It is said we be regenerated, but no man is regenerated of himself. And yet are not we regenerated as stocks, stones, or blocks; for we understand, we perceive, and we will: but it is God, which bringeth to pass that we understand, perceive and will. Wherefore there must be put a difference of men; for some be regenerate, and some be not. He that is not regenerate, can of himself do nothing: but after we be once regenerate, our strength is renewed, and we become workers together with God.

3. But in my judgment, we shall more easily understand what this phrase of God's repenting betokeneth, if we remember that his secret will is one, and his revealed will another: for the secret will of God is steadfast and immutable. Therefore, insomuch as it is said; God is not

changed; that ought to be referred to his secret will. God decreed from the beginning, that Saul should be king. That is his eternal and stable will, and without the which nothing is done. But he doth not always reveal the same full and wholly; it is enough that he showeth some part thereof through the law and the prophets. That will may be changed; not that there can any mutation happen unto God, but because that may be changed, which men thought would have continued forever. The revealed will of God was, that the kingdom should always be in the stock of Saul; for so it was like to have been: but yet the other part of his will was secret and hidden. Hezekiah falleth sick, Isaiah warneth him that he should die; for such was the nature of that disease, that it might seem he should die: this will was changed; the other which was secret, could not be changed.

But they object, that where we say; The will of God was from everlasting: it is but a mere devise; for that in God, there is nothing either past, or to come. But we allege nothing strange from the scriptures. Paul saith; that God hath predestinated us before the foundations of the world were laid. If they believe not us, let them look upon the prophesies. Jacob fore-showed that David should be king. How might this have been, unless the will of God have respect unto the time to come? But Paul in the 11th to the Romans saith; The gifts and calling of God are without repentance. But the sentences of the scriptures must not be more largely understood, than the place itself, wherein they be written, may bear: for otherwise we may be sooner lead to error. Paul entreated in that place of the covenant, which God made with the Jews, and saith, that these promises cannot be void; and that it cannot be, but that many of the Jews should be at length converted unto Christ, because The gifts and calling of God are without repentance. Although others understand that place as touching the gifts, which depend upon the eternal predestination of

God; for that they be sure and steadfast. Indeed other gifts, whether they belong to the justice of this life, or to things which be temporal, may both be given and taken away. For there be many, who having once believed, do afterward fall to destruction. Theodoretus saith; Gifts be without repentance, if the nature of the things themselves be considered: but if men fall from them, and be deprived of them, the fault is their own.

How it could be said to Saul, that his kingdom should be established forever, the same being before appointed to the tribe of Judah.

4. But let us see how Samuel said; The Lord would have established thy kingdom forever. For how could the kingdom have remained forever, in the family of Saul, seeing it was fore-told before of Jacob, that the kingdom should be in the tribe of Judah: and that God decreed from all eternity, that he would give the kingly right unto the house of David? Here we may not answer, that God indeed had so decreed at the first; but that he afterward changed his mind: for God is not changed. Rabbi Levi Ben Gerson thinketh, that this Hebrew word Adolam, signifieth not eternity, but some certain space of time; and that so Saul might reign, according to the meaning of that word Adolam, that is, for a long time, and afterward that David might succeed him. But this judgment I do not much allow; for David was now not only borne, but was also of ripe age, so as Saul might not reign for any long time. But that God is not changed, all men confess; yet all men not after one and the same manner: for some say, that we feign, that God doth predestinate somewhat from everlasting, which yet he executeth afterward. That (say they) is absurd; for all things are present unto God. Howbeit, we say not that God is moved for a time, but his counsels are from everlasting. But this we say, that when a thing is come to pass, he doth not appoint any new counsels.

Paul saith, that He was chosen from his mothers womb, and that we were predestinated before the foundations of the world. These things no doubt are everlasting in God, but in the things themselves they were pre-destinate long before they were made. But if they will cavil as touching predestination, we will object prophesies, in the which they cannot cavil; When they had done neither good nor evil, that the purpose of God, according to the election, might abide, it was said; Jacob have I loved, but Esau have I hated. So, as touching the kingdom to be established in the tribe of Judah, it was fore-showed long before David was borne, who first reigned in that tribe. How then doth Samuel say; God would have established thy kingdom forever? It is a potential manner of speaking. But what potency is this? There be also many such forms of speaking in the holy scriptures; If they had known (saith Paul) they would never have crucified the Lord of glory: but it was predestinated from the beginning, that Christ should die. So are they commonly wont to say; If Adam had not sinned, Christ had not suffered. But let us pass over those things, and let us examine that sentence which we have in hand, whereby the same being well understood, all other like may be understood.

5. And first let us see, whether the predestination of God touching David, were the cause why Saul was cast out of the kingdom. It seems to me that there were two causes of that casting out; one, the provoking of God, to wit, the sin of Saul; and the other was the will of God, but provoked and stirred up by sin: to which of these causes therefore shall we rather ascribe the casting out? Certainly, unto sin: for it was meet that he which had behaved himself ill, should be removed from his place. Therefore Oseas saith; Of the O Israel cometh thy evil. Indeed we cannot deny, but that the will of God was after some manner the cause; but the true and certain cause was sin. Also another, no small difference it shall be, if we compare our sins unto the punishments, and our good works unto the reward: for our sins deserve punishment, but good works deserve no reward, Why so wilt thou say? Because there is a proportion

between sin and punishment; but between good works and reward, there is none: for The passions of this life are not worthy of the glory to come, which shall be revealed unto us. Moreover, ill works are properly of our selves; but good works are not but of God. Wherefore eternal death may be called the reward of sin; but contrariwise, eternal life cannot be called the reward of our righteousness. So that we say, that the sin of Saul was the true cause why he fell from the kingdom; but his good works could never have been a cause for him to have continued. But whether did this counsel and decree lay a necessity upon Saul? Hereof there was no absolute necessity in him: for as touching the inward original of sinning, that had Saul in himself: and that which he did, he did it willingly, and of his own accord. Indeed God decreed the kingdom unto David, and to the tribe of Judah; but yet so, as the same should be first taken from him justly. And if God fore-saw that David should be king, he also fore-saw the sin of Saul: wherefore he saw the one thing and the other, both that the one should sin, and the other should reign: in this order there is no sin committed by God.

True indeed it is, that God might in such sort have punished Saul, as he would not take the kingdom from him. For he many ways punished the posterity of David, when they became idolaters; but yet he left the kingdom whole unto them. But it was in the hand of God to punish Saul after what manner he would: neither was the kingdom given to Saul, by the same covenant, that it was unto David. For when Jeroboam did invade Judah with four hundred thousand soldiers, Abias the king of Judah ascended unto a hill, and made an oration unto the ten tribes; Doo ye not know (saith he) that God gave the kingdom unto David with a covenant of salt? Salt doth not putrefy, nor suffereth corruption; further it was used in sacrifices. One thing [therein] signified that covenant made with David never to be violated; and another thing that the same was confirmed in a manner by sacrifice, and so now to become a holy thing. He did not so promise the kingdom unto Saul; for if he had promised it, it could not have been taken from him. Wherefore, although God had decreed these things as touching Saul and David, yet Saul sinned through originals in himself, and of his own accord. But if thou have a respect unto the foreknowledge of God, some necessity indeed is in it; but yet (as they say) by supposition only, for the fore-knowledge of God cannot be deceived. But yet God interrupteth not the course of things, but suffereth that whatsoever is done, is doon naturally, and of his own accord.

6. But come we nearer; He would have established thy kingdom forever. How? Because he would have ordained, by an everlasting decree, that his kingdom should have abiden with his posterity forever: and so this power shall stand in the decree of God. Over this, so far as concerneth the nature of Saul, God might have established unto him the kingdom forever; which we perceive was done in other kings, whom God cast not out when they had sinned. But there is another solution far more easy; to say, that these things were spoken after the manner of men: for men are wont to say, that something is done, or may be done, when it appeareth to be done, or seemeth that it may be done. For so Christ speaketh, when he saith; Rejoice and be glad, because your names be written in heaven, and yet in the meantime Judas was there, and the seventy disciples were there, who afterward departed from Christ. How then were their names written in heaven? Because so they seemed to be, and of those principles they had now a beginning. So it is written in the Apocalypse; Hold thy place, least another receive thy crown. How was that a crown, which might be forgone? Because unto men so it seemed to be; and because they used those outward means, whereby we come unto the crown. For the crown is either of predestination, and that is certain and cannot be

lost; or else of inchoation; or else because so it may seem to be, and that may be prevented.

Of the crown which may seem to be, thus Christ speaketh; From him that hath not shall be taken away, even that which he seemeth to have. He saith not; That which he hath, but only that which he seemeth to have. And of inchoation it is written to the Hebrews; They which where once lightened, and have tasted the good word of God, &c: those men, as touching these means, seem to have the crown; but if they fall away (saith Paul) they cannot be renewed. So the kingdom of Saul might have been established forever, because it had that beginning, and those means, by which a kingdom might have been retained. So Matthias was substitute in the place of Judas, Seth in the place of Abel, the Gentiles in the place of the Jews. So Job saith in the 24th chapter; God shall consume many and mighty nations, and shall set others in their places. So when the angels fell, men succeeded in their place. And in the prophet Jeremiah, the sense of this place is this; If I shall pronounce evil as touching any nation, and that nation shall repent, I also will repent me of all the evil, which I was purposed to do. The promise made to Saul, as touching the kingdom, had a condition; whereunto when he stood not, the kingdom by good right was taken from him.

Of Temptation.

7. The etymology of the word cometh of [the Hebrew word] Nas, which is, A sign or token; for Nasa, which signifieth, To tempt, is then certainly done, when we would know anything by some certain sign or token: the Grecians call it "πεῖρα" (peira), which is Experience. Let us define it; Temptation is a thorough search for getting out the knowledge of an unknown thing. The formal cause is action; the end knowledge, of many things doubtless, of man's own self, of weakness or strength, of God's divine goodness or wrath. But knowledge is not the principal end;

because in godly men, the end is oftentimes, that they may vanquish and be crowned; or if they be fallen, they being raised up again by the help of God, may be humbled, and become more diligent in the service and religion of God. The matter wherein it is, is our mind; and it is conversant about all vices, the which, as to their own head, are reduced to infidelity. The efficient cause thereof (no doubt) is the flesh, the world, and the devil. But the controversy is as touching God, whether it may be ascribed unto him.

8. This doth James seem to deny, when he saith; that Every man is tempted by his own proper concupiscence, and the God is no tempter of evil things. And Paul seemeth to consent thereunto, at the leastwise that all temptations proceed not of God: for he saith, that he with temptations maketh a way to get out. But there be many temptations, wherein poor souls be catched; neither is there any way for them to escape, yea rather they perish in them. Besides this, we cannot perceive by any reason, how it comes to pass, that God can punish sins; and yet by tempting is become an author of them. But all this notwithstanding, we must lean surly to the holy scriptures, which everywhere ascribe temptation unto God. In the eight of Deuteronomy thou readest, that God tempted the children of Israel in the desert, that he might know whether they would keep his commandments or no: in which place thou hast the end of temptation. In the psalm David prayeth, that The Lord would tempt him. Job was tempted, God delivering him unto Satan. In the first of Samuel thou findest, that the wicked spirit invaded Saul, and moved him to depart from God. And David, in the second of Samuel, was stirred up by Satan to number the people; but in the 21st of Chronicles, it is said, that God stirred up David against Israel: wherefore one and the same action is attributed unto God, and unto Satan. We have also a plain place concerning Abraham. Ahab is seduced by the will of God, who sent a

spirit to be a liar in the mouth of the prophets; God hardened the heart of Pharaoh. In the first of Isaiah the prophet is sent to preach, that They seeing should not perceive; that their eyes should be shut, and their heart hardened, least peradventure (saith he) they should be converted, and I might heal them: God sendeth his word unto them for a snare. And in Isaiah the 63rd chapter; The fathers complain (saying) Wherefore hast thou led us out of the way? Wherefore hast thou made our heart to err from thy ways? Christ said unto Philip; Whence shall we buy bread? He knew what he would do: but so he spake, tempting him. And we pray to God our father, saying; Lead us not into temptation.

There be some, which would thus resolve the doubt; God tempteth, (that is to say) he suffereth and permitteth to tempt. But this prevaileth nothing, we must not shun the phrase of the scriptures. If the scripture speak thus, why should not we also speak it? Moreover, this cannot expound all the places of scripture alleged by us: for the Lord himself sent Isaiah, and God himself sent the lying spirit unto Ahab; neither was Abraham tempted by any other than by God. Add also, that in permission there is the will of God; and seeing it is manifest concerning the thing itself, what doth the changing of the word profit? But go to, let us see what ill comes of it, if tempting be attributed unto God. Verily no evil, nay rather it is meet for him, and it becometh his nature, who endeavoreth to reveal his righteousness and mercy in all things. They that be tempted, do belong either unto the chosen, or unto the damned; either they be godly, or else ungodly. If [they be] ungodly, as their sins may be punished with other sins (which is declared in the first chapter to the Romans) so they may be punished with temptations, that through them they may fall headlong into diverse evils, whereby they may be judged worthy of everlasting punishment. If [they be] godly, God by tempting them declareth and testifieth what account he maketh of them; he is present forthwith, he delivereth them, crowneth them, and rewardeth them like conquerors, with many and honorable gifts: or else if they fall, that fall is but for a time, and at last (even as Paul said) it hath an happy issue. Thereby their faith, hope, and charity is increased, while they perceive themselves to be holpen, and by the great favor of God to overcome their enemies: or else because they be lightened from the burden of their sins.

9. But in the meantime let us make answer to those reasons, which seemed to persuade us otherwise. James, when he denieth that God doth tempt, doth not utterly deny it; but he denieth him to tempt after that manner, which those carnal Christians of his time affirmed him to tempt: as who should say, when they sinned, they should have been without blame: as our Libertines are reported to say at this day, namely that God doth all things in us; and that therefore sin is nothing: no not robberies, murders, adulteries, and such like. Indeed we grant, that God doth all things; but the respect of God's doing, and our doing of them is diverse. Men, in that they do those things, they sin; as they which are not led unto those things of an intent that they may work together with God; neither are they constrained or compelled unto those things against their wills; nay rather, they would be angry with them that should let them from sinning. Wherefore let them ask their own conscience, and then they shall plainly see, whether they sin against their will, or to the intent they may gratify God; or else not rather to satisfy their own unbridled lust.

Now by the like reason saith James, God doth not so tempt you, as the cause and fault of those things, which ye do naughtily and wickedly, should be laid against him. Ye be tempted by your own concupiscence; that is, ye therefore fall into your own wickedness, to the intent ye may satisfy your greedy lust. Wherefore that which the apostle there meant, and would in some respect to be denied, he uttered by an absolute denial. But Paul, when he saith, that God maketh a way to escape with the temptation, certainly he speaketh of those temptations, wherewith the godly and elect are sometimes vexed; whereby doubtless they have for the most part, not only an escaping, but also a reward. But in that we do not so well perceive, how it is not repugnant with the justice of God, to punish sins, and to drive [men] unto them by tempting, that is no marvel; for God can do more than we can understand. David said once, as touching the knowing of these secret judgments in the 73rd psalm; that he was very pensive, and that his grief was intolerable, until he entered into the sanctuary of God. Wherefore let us constantly believe, that whatsoever God doth, he doth it justly; neither let us withdraw from his providence or power, any of those things that be done: but if we understand not how they be agreeable unto his justice, or how they be repugnant therewith, let us with humility believe.

10. But let us proceed. Since they be of God, whether may we pray to be rid of them? Let us distinguish temptations; either they be adversities, or else they be suggestions unto wicked deeds: if they be adversities, we must not pray to be pressed with no adversities, seeing it is plainly told us by Paul; They that will live godly in Christ must suffer persecutions. And Christ offereth the cross unto his to be borne, in a manner all their life long: but if we doubt of fainting in those persecutions, or that the glory of God be hindered by them, we may pray, that he will remove them from us. Paul prayed, and would have it prayed for, that he might be delivered from the persecutions, which were ready for him in Jury. Moreover, if our flesh be frail, while affliction lasteth, and we pray the father devoutly, that he will deliver us, if it be his pleasure; yet nevertheless, in preferring his will before our own will, we offend not by such a request: which thing Christ taught us, when he prayed to his father in the garden. But

if we consider the saints, while they constantly, through the grace of God, behave themselves in these temptations, we shall perceive, that they rejoice in them; for Tribulation worketh patience, patience experience. And Peter in the first chapter of his first epistle, saith; that There is joy to the saints in temptations: yea and Paul doth glory in his adversities. The which he meaneth not, as they proceed from the devil, or from wicked men; but as they come from the providence of God, and be the instruments of his reward and salvation. But if they tend unto evil, that is, that they be provocations unto sin, then must they be distinguished; because therein is either fall or victory. If victory be joined with them, this kind is desired of saints; to the intent the devil, the flesh, and the world, may every day more and more be vanquished in them. But if they be afraid of falling, it is either temporal or eternal: if it be temporal, we must pray for the avoiding of temptation, as we do in the Lord's prayer; And lead us not into temptation.

This did Christ teach his apostles, when he said; The spirit indeed is ready, but the flesh is frail: watch and pray, that ye enter not into temptation. And reason leadeth us thereunto; for we ought to detest all things that are contrary unto the will of God, such is a fall against the law of God: yea nothing ought to be more displeasing unto us, even as it appeareth by the commandment; Thou shalt love the Lord, with all thine heart, and with all thy soul. To these things add, that none ought to have such confidence in his own strength, as he should not fear in temptation. Wherefore in temptation we must always pray, but not that we may not be tempted at all, seeing God hath appointed our life to be a warfare. But godly men are not afraid of temptations, which have a perpetual and deadly end; for they know, that God is a father unto them: which they would not believe, if they misdoubted that they should be forsaken of him. Further, they acknowledge, that The calling and gifts of God are without repentance, as it is said in the epistle to the Romans.

www.ingramcontent.com/pod-product-compliance
Lightning Source LLC
Chambersburg PA
CBHW042316120626
46547CB00022B/2112

* 9 7 8 1 9 6 1 8 0 7 7 5 4 *